Data Science with SQL Server Quick Start Guide

Integrate SQL Server with data science

Dejan Sarka

BIRMINGHAM - MUMBAI

Data Science with SQL Server Quick Start Guide

Copyright © 2018 Packt Publishing

Commissioning Editor: Amey Varangaonkar
Acquisition Editor: Reshma Raman
Content Development Editor: Roshan Kumar
Technical Editor: Sushmeeta Jena
Copy Editor: Safis Editing
Project Coordinator: Hardik Bhinde
Proofreader: Safis Editing
Indexer: Aishwarya Gangawane
Graphics: Jason Monteiro
Production Coordinator: Shraddha Falebhai

First published: August 2018

Production reference: 1300818

Published by Packt Publishing Ltd.
Livery Place
35 Livery Street
Birmingham
B3 2PB, UK.

ISBN 978-1-78953-712-3

www.packtpub.com

`mapt.io`

Mapt is an online digital library that gives you full access to over 5,000 books and videos, as well as industry leading tools to help you plan your personal development and advance your career. For more information, please visit our website.

Why subscribe?

- Spend less time learning and more time coding with practical eBooks and Videos from over 4,000 industry professionals

- Improve your learning with Skill Plans built especially for you

- Get a free eBook or video every month

- Mapt is fully searchable

- Copy and paste, print, and bookmark content

PacktPub.com

Did you know that Packt offers eBook versions of every book published, with PDF and ePub files available? You can upgrade to the eBook version at `www.PacktPub.com` and as a print book customer, you are entitled to a discount on the eBook copy. Get in touch with us at `service@packtpub.com` for more details.

At `www.PacktPub.com`, you can also read a collection of free technical articles, sign up for a range of free newsletters, and receive exclusive discounts and offers on Packt books and eBooks.

Contributors

About the author

Dejan Sarka, MCT and Microsoft Data Platform MVP, is an independent trainer and consultant who focuses on the development of database and business intelligence applications. Besides projects, he spends about half his time on training and mentoring. He is the founder of the Slovenian SQL Server and .NET Users Group. He is the main author or co author of many books about databases and SQL Server. The last three books before this one were published by Packt, and their titles were *SQL Server 2016 Developer's Guide, SQL Server 2017 Integration Services Cookbook*, and *SQL Server 2016 Developer's Guide*. Dejan Sarka has also developed many courses and seminars for Microsoft, SolidQ, and Pluralsight.

I would like to thank to all of the wonderful people that made the writing process as smooth as possible. Without their enormous contribution, the writing would have been a very hard job for me. Special thanks goes to the content editors, Aditi Gour and Roshan Kumar. Tomaž Kaštrun reviewed my work a third time. As always, he was precise and constant. Thank you, Tomaž.

Finally, I want to thank my significant other, who has put up with me for more than 30 years.

About the reviewer

Tomaz Kastrun is an SQL Server developer and data scientist with more than 15 years, experience in the fields of business warehousing, development, ETL, database administration, and also data analysis and machine learning. He is a Microsoft Data Platform MVP, a blogger, and a frequent speaker at community and Microsoft events. When he is not working, drinking coffee, or riding a fixed-gear bike, he enjoys spending time with his daughter, Rubi.

> *I would like to express my deepest gratitude to my colleague, friend, and community leader, the author of this book, Dejan Sarka, for his immense work and the energy he brings to the SQL community every day, and for all the passion he puts into his work, sharing his wisdom and wit. Thank you.*

Packt is searching for authors like you

If you're interested in becoming an author for Packt, please visit `authors.packtpub.com` and apply today. We have worked with thousands of developers and tech professionals, just like you, to help them share their insight with the global tech community. You can make a general application, apply for a specific hot topic that we are recruiting an author for, or submit your own idea.

Table of Contents

Preface

The book will give you a jump-start in data science with Microsoft SQL Server and in-database Machine Learning Services (ML Services). It covers all stages of a data science project, from business and data understanding through data overview, data preparation, and modeling, to using algorithms, model evaluation, and deployment. The book shows how to use the engines and languages that come with SQL Server, including ML Services with R, Python, and Transact-SQL (T-SQL). You will find useful code examples in all three languages mentioned. The book also shows which algorithms to use for which tasks, and briefly explains each algorithm.

Who this book is for

SQL Server only started to fully support data science with its two latest versions, 2016 and 2017. Therefore, SQL Server is not widely used for data science yet. However, there are professionals from the worlds of SQL Server and data science who are interested in using SQL Server and ML Services for their projects. Therefore, this book is intended for SQL Server professionals who want to start with data science, and data scientists who would like to start using SQL Server in their projects.

What this book covers

Chapter 1, *Writing Queries with T-SQL*, gives a brief overview of T-SQL queries. It introduces all of the important parts of the mighty SELECT statement and focuses on analytical queries.

Chapter 2, *Introducing R*, introduces the second language in this book, R. R has been supported in SQL Server since version 2016. In order to use it properly, you have to understand the language constructs and data structures.

Chapter 3, *Getting Familiar with Python*, gives an overview of the second most popular data science language, Python. As a more general language, Python is probably even more popular than R. Lately, Python has been catching up with R in the data science field.

Chapter 4, *Data Overview*, deals with understanding data. You can use introductory statistics and basic graphs for this task. You will learn how to perform a data overview in all three languages used in this book.

Chapter 5, *Data Preparation,* teaches you how to work with the data that you get from your business systems and from data warehouses, which is typically not suited for direct use in a machine learning project. You need to add derived variables, deal with outliers and missing values, and more.

Chapter 6, *Intermediate Statistics and Graphs,* starts with the real analysis of the data. You can use intermediate-level statistical methods and graphs for the beginning of your advanced analytics journey.

Chapter 7, *Unsupervised Machine Learning,* explains the algorithms that do not use a target variable. It is like fishing in the mud - you try and see if some meaningful information can be extracted from your data. The most common undirected techniques are clustering, dimensionality reduction, and affinity grouping, also known as basket analysis or association rules.

Chapter 8, *Supervised Machine Learning,* deals with the algorithms that need a target variable. Some of the most important directed techniques include classification and estimation. Classification means examining a new case and assigning it to a predefined discrete class, for example, assigning keywords to articles and assigning customers to known segments. Next is estimation, where you try to estimate the value of a continuous variable of a new case. You can, for example, estimate the number of children or the family income. This chapter also shows you how you can evaluate your machine learning models and use them for predictions.

To get the most out of this book

In order to run the demo code associated with this book, you will need SQL Server 2017, SQL Server Management Studio, and Visual Studio 2017.

All of the information about the installation of the software needed to run the code is included in the first three chapters of the book.

Download the example code files

You can download the example code files for this book from your account at www.packtpub.com. If you purchased this book elsewhere, you can visit www.packtpub.com/support and register to have the files emailed directly to you.

You can download the code files by following these steps:

1. Log in or register at `www.packtpub.com`.
2. Select the **SUPPORT** tab.
3. Click on **Code Downloads & Errata**.
4. Enter the name of the book in the **Search** box and follow the onscreen instructions.

Once the file is downloaded, please make sure that you unzip or extract the folder using the latest version of:

- WinRAR/7-Zip for Windows
- Zipeg/iZip/UnRarX for Mac
- 7-Zip/PeaZip for Linux

The code bundle for the book is also hosted on GitHub at `https://github.com/PacktPublishing/Data-Science-with-SQL-Server-Quick-Start-Guide`. In case there's an update to the code, it will be updated on the existing GitHub repository.

We also have other code bundles from our rich catalog of books and videos available at `https://github.com/PacktPublishing/`. Check them out!

Download the color images

We also provide a PDF file that has color images of the screenshots/diagrams used in this book. You can download it here: `http://www.packtpub.com/sites/default/files/downloads/DataSciencewithSQLServerQuickStartGuide_ColorImages.pdf`.

Conventions used

There are a number of text conventions used throughout this book.

`CodeInText`: Indicates code words in text, database table names, folder names, filenames, file extensions, pathnames, dummy URLs, user input, and Twitter handles. Here is an example: "Mount the downloaded `WebStorm-10*.dmg` disk image file as another disk in your system."

A block of code is set as follows:

```
# R version and contributors
R.version.string
contributors()
```

When we wish to draw your attention to a particular part of a code block, the relevant lines or items are set in bold:

```
1 + 2
2 + 5 * 4
3 ^ 4
sqrt(81)
pi
```

Any command-line input or output is written as follows:

```
install.packages("RODBC")
library(RODBC)
```

Bold: Indicates a new term, an important word, or words that you see onscreen. For example, words in menus or dialog boxes appear in the text like this. Here is an example: "Select **System info** from the **Administration** panel."

Warnings or important notes appear like this.

Tips and tricks appear like this.

Get in touch

Feedback from our readers is always welcome.

General feedback: Email feedback@packtpub.com and mention the book title in the subject of your message. If you have questions about any aspect of this book, please email us at questions@packtpub.com.

Errata: Although we have taken every care to ensure the accuracy of our content, mistakes do happen. If you have found a mistake in this book, we would be grateful if you would report this to us. Please visit www.packtpub.com/submit-errata, selecting your book, clicking on the Errata Submission Form link, and entering the details.

Piracy: If you come across any illegal copies of our works in any form on the Internet, we would be grateful if you would provide us with the location address or website name. Please contact us at copyright@packtpub.com with a link to the material.

If you are interested in becoming an author: If there is a topic that you have expertise in and you are interested in either writing or contributing to a book, please visit authors.packtpub.com.

Reviews

Please leave a review. Once you have read and used this book, why not leave a review on the site that you purchased it from? Potential readers can then see and use your unbiased opinion to make purchase decisions, we at Packt can understand what you think about our products, and our authors can see your feedback on their book. Thank you!

For more information about Packt, please visit packtpub.com.

Writing Queries with T-SQL

1

This book is intended for any SQL Server developer or **database administrator (DBA)** who wants to start working in the data science field. In addition, this book is also aimed at existing data scientists who want to start using SQL Server with related services and tools. I will use, and show examples in, three programming languages in this book: **Transact-SQL** (or **T-SQL**), **R**, and **Python**. Therefore, it makes sense to start with a brief introduction of the three languages. This is what the first three chapters are about. If you are already a SQL Server developer, proficient in writing T-SQL queries, you can simply skip the first chapter. If you are already working with R, skip the second chapter. If you are familiar with Python, please feel free to skip the third chapter.

This first chapter is not a comprehensive reference guide to T-SQL; I will focus on the mighty `SELECT` statement only, the statement you need to use immediately when your data is located in a SQL Server database. However, besides the basic clauses, I will also explain advanced techniques, such as window functions, common table expressions, and the `APPLY` operator.

This chapter will cover the following points:

- Core Transact-SQL SELECT statement elements
- Advanced SELECT techniques

Before starting – installing SQL Server

If you don't have a SQL Server yet, you can use a free SQL Server Evaluation Edition or Developer Edition. You can download any of them from the SQL Server downloads site at `https://www.microsoft.com/en-ca/sql-server/sql-server-downloads`.

SQL Server setup

You just start SQL Server setup, and then from the **Feature Selection** page select the following:

- **Database Engine Services**
- Underneath **Machine Learning** (ML) **Services (In-Database)**
- With both languages, **R** and **Python**, selected, like you can see in the next screenshot

After that, all you need is client tools, and you can start writing the code. The following screenshot shows the SQL Server setup **Feature Selection** page with the appropriate features selected:

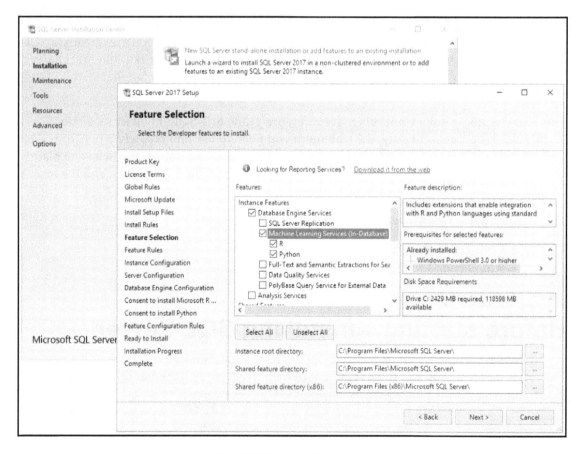

Figure 1.1: SQL Server Setup feature selection

The next step is to install client tools. Of course, you need **SQL Server Management Studio (SSMS)**. You can download it at `https://docs.microsoft.com/en-us/sql/ssms/download-sql-server-management-studio-ssms?view=sql-server-2017`. If you are not familiar with this tool, please use the SSMS at `https://docs.microsoft.com/en-us/sql/ssms/tutorials/tutorial-sql-server-management-studio?view=sql-server-2017` to learn the basics about this tool.

 In the next two chapters, I will explain what other tools you need to efficiently write R and Python code, respectively.

Finally, you need some demo data. I will mostly use the `AdventureWorksDW2017` demo database in this book. You can find this demo database and other Microsoft samples at `https://github.com/Microsoft/sql-server-samples/releases`. I will point you to the appropriate sources when I use any other demo data in this book.

After you install everything mentioned so for, you are ready to start learning or renewing the knowledge of the T-SQL `SELECT` statement.

Core T-SQL SELECT statement elements

You probably already know that the most important SQL statement is the mighty `SELECT` statement you use to retrieve data from your databases. Every database developer knows the basic clauses and their usage:

- `SELECT`: Defines the columns returned, or a projection of all table columns
- `FROM`: Lists the tables used in the query and how they are associated, or joined
- `WHERE`: Filters the data to return only the rows that satisfy the condition in the predicate
- `GROUP BY`: Defines the groups over which the data is aggregated
- `HAVING`: Filters the data after the grouping with conditions that refer to aggregations
- `ORDER BY`: Sorts the rows returned to the client application

The simplest form of the SELECT statement

Let's start with the simplest concept of SQL that every Tom, Dick, and Harry is aware of!
The simplest query to retrieve the data you can write includes the SELECT and the FROM
clauses. In the select clause, you can use the star character, literally SELECT *, to denote
that you need all columns from a table in the result set. The following code switches to the
AdventureWorksDW2017 database context and selects all data from the dbo.DimEmployee
table:

```
USE AdventureWorksDW2017;
GO
SELECT *
FROM dbo.DimEmployee;
```

This query returns 296 rows, all employees with all columns.

 Using SELECT * is not recommended in production. Queries
with SELECT * can return an unexpected result when the table structure
changes and are also not suitable for good optimization.

Better than using SELECT * is to explicitly list only the columns you need. This means you
are returning only a projection on the table. The following example selects only three
columns from the table:

```
SELECT EmployeeKey, FirstName, LastName
FROM dbo.DimEmployee;
```

Here is the shortened result, limited to the first three rows only:

```
EmployeeKey FirstName LastName
----------- --------- ----------
1           Guy       Gilbert
2           Kevin     Brown
3           Roberto   Tamburello
```

Object names in SQL Server, such as table and column, can include spaces. Names that
include spaces are called **delimited identifiers**. To make SQL Server properly understand
them as column names, you must enclose delimited identifiers in square brackets.
However, if you prefer to have names without spaces, or if you use computed expressions
in the column list, you can add column aliases. The following code uses an expression in
the SELECT clause to create a calculated column called [Full Name], and then uses the
INTO clause to store the data in a table.

The next query retrieves the data from the newly created and populated `dbo.EmpFull` table:

```
SELECT EmployeeKey,
 FirstName + ' ' + LastName AS [Full Name]
INTO dbo.EmpFUll
FROM dbo.DimEmployee;
GO
SELECT EmployeeKey, [Full Name]
FROM dbo.EmpFUll;
```

Here is the partial result:

```
EmployeeKey Full Name
----------- ------------------
1           Guy Gilbert
2           Kevin Brown
3           Roberto Tamburello
```

As you have seen before, there are 296 employees. If you check the full result of the first query, you might notice that there is a column named `SalesPersonFlag` in the `dbo.DimEmployee` table. You might want to check which of the employees are also salespeople. You can filter the results of a query with the `WHERE` clause, as the following query shows:

```
SELECT EmployeeKey, FirstName, LastName
FROM dbo.DimEmployee
WHERE SalesPersonFlag = 1;
```

This query returns 17 rows only.

Joining multiple tables

In a relational database, you typically have data spread in multiple tables. Each table represents a set of entities of the same kind, such as employees in the examples you have seen so far. In order to make result sets meaningful for the business your database supports, most of the time you need to retrieve data from multiple tables in the same query. You need to join two or more tables based on some conditions. The most frequent kind of a join is the inner join. An inner join returns only rows for which the condition in the join predicate for the two joined tables evaluates to true. Note that in a relational database, you have three-valued logic, because there is always a possibility that a piece of data is unknown. You mark the unknown with the `NULL` keyword. A predicate can thus evaluate to true, false, or NULL. For an inner join, the order of the tables involved in the join is not important.

In the following example, you can see the `dbo.DimEmployee` table joined with an inner join to the `dbo.FactResellerSales` table:

```
SELECT e.EmployeeKey, e.FirstName, e.LastName,
 fr.SalesAmount
FROM dbo.DimEmployee AS e
 INNER JOIN dbo.FactResellerSales AS fr
  ON e.EmployeeKey = fr.EmployeeKey;
```

Here are the partial results:

```
EmployeeKey FirstName LastName SalesAmount
----------- --------- -------- -----------
285         Tsvi      Reiter   2024.994
285         Tsvi      Reiter   6074.982
285         Tsvi      Reiter   2024.994
```

In the previous query, you can see that table aliases are used. If a column's name is unique across all tables in the query, you can use it without a table name. If not, you need to use table name in front of the column, to avoid ambiguous column names, in the `table.column` format. In the previous query, the `EmployeeKey` column appears in both tables. Therefore, you need to precede this column name with the table name of its origin to avoid ambiguity. You can shorten the two-part column names by using table aliases. You specify table aliases in the FROM clause. Once you specify table aliases, you must always use the aliases; you can't refer to the original table names in that query anymore. Please note that a column name might be unique in the query at the moment when you write the query. However, later somebody could add a column with the same name in another table involved in the query. If the column name is not preceded by an alias or by the table name, you would get an error when executing the query because of the ambiguous column name. In order to make the code more stable and more readable, you should always use table aliases for each column in the query.

The previous query returned 60,855 rows. It is always recommended to know at least approximately the number of rows your query should return. This number is the first control of the correctness of the result set, or said differently, whether the query is written in a logically correct way. If every sale has an employee, as it should have, then the previous query should have returned exactly the number of rows `dbo.FactResellerSales` has. You can quickly check the number of rows in the `dbo.FactResellerSales` table with the help of the COUNT (*) aggregate function, as the following query shows:

```
SELECT COUNT(*) AS ResellerSalesCount
FROM dbo.FactResellerSales;
```

The result is, as you probably expected, 60,855 rows.

You can join multiple tables in a single query. The following code joins seven tables in a single query. Note that all of the joins are still inner joins. The query returns 60,855 rows again, with at least 1 column from each table involved in the query:

```
SELECT e.EmployeeKey, e.FirstName, e.LastName,
 r.ResellerKey, r.ResellerName,
 d.DateKey, d.CalendarYear, d.CalendarQuarter,
 p.ProductKey, p.EnglishProductName,
 ps.EnglishProductSubcategoryName,
 pc.EnglishProductCategoryName,
 fr.OrderQuantity, fr.SalesAmount
FROM dbo.DimEmployee AS e
 INNER JOIN dbo.FactResellerSales AS fr
  ON e.EmployeeKey = fr.EmployeeKey
 INNER JOIN dbo.DimReseller AS r
  ON r.ResellerKey = fr.ResellerKey
 INNER JOIN dbo.DimDate AS d
  ON fr.OrderDateKey = d.DateKey
 INNER JOIN dbo.DimProduct AS p
  ON fr.ProductKey = p.ProductKey
 INNER JOIN dbo.DimProductSubcategory AS ps
  ON p.ProductSubcategoryKey = ps.ProductSubcategoryKey
 INNER JOIN dbo.DimProductCategory AS pc
  ON ps.ProductCategoryKey = pc.ProductCategoryKey;
```

In the dbo.Employees table, there are 17 salespeople. Do all of them have at least one sale, at least one row from the dbo.FactResellerSales table associated with the employee key of that salesperson? You can check how many distinct employees have sales associated with them with the help of the DISTINCT keyword:

```
SELECT DISTINCT fr.EmployeeKey
FROM dbo.FactResellerSales AS fr;
```

The query returns 17 rows. Now imagine that you would like to list all sales rows together with the employees' data, but you also need to include in the result the employees that are not salespeople, that do now have any row associated with their EmployeeKey column in the fact table. You can use an outer join to fulfill this task.

With an outer join, you preserve the rows from one or both tables, even if they don't have a match in the other table. The result set returned includes all of the matched rows, like what you get from an inner join plus the preserved rows. Within an outer join, the order of the tables involved in the join might be important. If you use LEFT OUTER JOIN, the rows from the left table are preserved. If you use RIGHT OUTER JOIN, the rows from the right table are preserved. Of course, in both cases, the order of the tables involved in the join is important. With FULL OUTER JOIN, you preserve the rows from both tables, and the order of the tables is not important. The following query uses a left outer join to preserve the rows from the dbo.DimEmployee table:

```
SELECT e.EmployeeKey, e.FirstName, e.LastName,
 fr.SalesAmount
FROM dbo.DimEmployee AS e
 LEFT OUTER JOIN dbo.FactResellerSales AS fr
  ON e.EmployeeKey = fr.EmployeeKey;
```

The query returns 61,134 rows. Did we get all of the employees in the result? You can check this by checking the distinct EmployeeKey after the outer join:

```
SELECT DISTINCT e.EmployeeKey
FROM dbo.DimEmployee AS e
 LEFT OUTER JOIN dbo.FactResellerSales AS fr
  ON e.EmployeeKey = fr.EmployeeKey;
```

The query returns 296 rows, which is the number of employees.

Joining more than two tables is not tricky if all of the joins are inner joins. The order of joins is not important. However, you might want to execute an outer join after all of the inner joins. If you don't control the join order with the outer joins, it might happen that a subsequent inner join filters out the preserved rows of an outer join. You can control the join order with parentheses. The following query uses the right outer join to preserve all employees and makes sure that this join is executed after all inner joins:

```
SELECT e.EmployeeKey, e.FirstName, e.LastName,
 r.ResellerKey, r.ResellerName,
 d.DateKey, d.CalendarYear, d.CalendarQuarter,
 p.ProductKey, p.EnglishProductName,
 ps.EnglishProductSubcategoryName,
 pc.EnglishProductCategoryName,
 fr.OrderQuantity, fr.SalesAmount
FROM (dbo.FactResellerSales AS fr
 INNER JOIN dbo.DimReseller AS r
  ON r.ResellerKey = fr.ResellerKey
 INNER JOIN dbo.DimDate AS d
  ON fr.OrderDateKey = d.DateKey
 INNER JOIN dbo.DimProduct AS p
```

```
  ON fr.ProductKey = p.ProductKey
INNER JOIN dbo.DimProductSubcategory AS ps
  ON p.ProductSubcategoryKey = ps.ProductSubcategoryKey
INNER JOIN dbo.DimProductCategory AS pc
  ON ps.ProductCategoryKey = pc.ProductCategoryKey)
RIGHT OUTER JOIN dbo.DimEmployee AS e
  ON e.EmployeeKey = fr.EmployeeKey;
```

The query returns 61,134 rows, as it should. Note that with the usage of the parenthesis, the order of joins is defined in the following way:

- Perform all inner joins, with an arbitrary order among them

- Execute the left outer join after all of the inner joins

Grouping and aggregating data

Many times, you need to aggregate data in groups. This is where the GROUP BY clause comes in handy. The following query aggregates the sales data for each employee:

```
SELECT e.EmployeeKey,
  MIN(e.LastName) AS LastName,
  SUM(fr.OrderQuantity)AS EmpTotalQuantity,
  SUM(fr.SalesAmount) AS EmpTotalAmount
FROM dbo.DimEmployee AS e
  INNER JOIN dbo.FactResellerSales AS fr
    ON e.EmployeeKey = fr.EmployeeKey
GROUP BY e.EmployeeKey;
```

The query returns 17 aggregated rows. Here are the results, abbreviated to the first three rows only:

```
EmployeeKey LastName    EmpTotalQuantity EmpTotalAmount
----------- ----------  ---------------- --------------
284         Vargas      11544            3609447.2163
295         Valdez      6898             1790640.2311
281         Blythe      23058            9293903.0055
```

In the SELECT clause, you can have only the columns used for grouping, or aggregated columns. That is why the LastName column in the SELECT list is used in the MIN() aggregate function. You need to get a scalar, a single aggregated value for each row for each column not included in the GROUP BY list.

Sometimes, you need to filter aggregated data. For example, you might need to find only the employees for which the sum of the order quantity did not reach 10,000. You can filter the result set on the aggregated data by using the HAVING clause:

```
SELECT e.EmployeeKey,
 MIN(e.LastName) AS LastName,
 SUM(fr.OrderQuantity)AS EmpTotalQuantity,
 SUM(fr.SalesAmount) AS EmpTotalAmount
FROM dbo.DimEmployee AS e
 INNER JOIN dbo.FactResellerSales AS fr
  ON e.EmployeeKey = fr.EmployeeKey
GROUP BY e.EmployeeKey
HAVING SUM(fr.OrderQuantity) < 10000;
```

The query returns eight rows only. Note that you can't use column aliases from the SELECT clause in any other clause introduced in the previous query. The SELECT clause logically executes after all other clauses from the query, and the aliases are not known yet. However, the ORDER BY clause, which sorts the result, executes after the SELECT clause, and therefore the columns aliases are already known and you can refer to them. The following query shows the nine employees with sum of the OrderQuantity variable greater than 10,000, sorted in descending order by this sum:

```
SELECT e.EmployeeKey,
 MIN(e.LastName) AS LastName,
 SUM(fr.OrderQuantity)AS EmpTotalQuantity,
 SUM(fr.SalesAmount) AS EmpTotalAmount
FROM dbo.DimEmployee AS e
 INNER JOIN dbo.FactResellerSales AS fr
  ON e.EmployeeKey = fr.EmployeeKey
GROUP BY e.EmployeeKey
HAVING SUM(fr.OrderQuantity) > 10000
ORDER BY EmpTotalQuantity DESC;
```

You can see the shortened results as follows:

```
EmployeeKey LastName    EmpTotalQuantity EmpTotalAmount
----------- ---------- ---------------- --------------
282         Mitchell   27229            10367007.4286
283         Carson     27051            10065803.5429
291         Pak        26231            8503338.6472
```

Advanced SELECT techniques

Aggregating data over the complete input rowset or aggregating in groups produces aggregated rows only, either one row for the whole input rowset or one row per group. Sometimes, you need to return aggregates together with the detail data. One way to achieve this is by using subqueries, which are queries inside queries.

Introducing subqueries

The next query shows an example of using two subqueries in a single query: in the SELECT clause, a subquery that calculates the sum of quantity for each employee. It returns a scalar value. The subquery refers to the employee key from the outer query. The subquery can't execute without the outer query. This is a correlated subquery. There is another subquery in the FROM clause that calculates the overall quantity for all employees. This query returns a table, although it is a table with a single row and a single column. This query is a self-contained subquery, independent of the outer query. A subquery in the FROM clause is also called a derived table.

Another type of join is used to add the overall total to each detail row. A cross-join is a Cartesian product of two input rowsets: each row from one side is associated with every single row from the other side. No join condition is needed. A cross-join can produce an unwanted, huge result set. For example, if you cross-join just 1,000 rows from the left side of the join with 1,000 rows from the right side, you get 1,000,000 rows in the output. Therefore, typically you want to avoid a cross-join in production. However, in the example in the following query, 60,855 from the left-side rows is cross-joined to a single row from the subquery, therefore producing only 60,855. Effectively, this means that the overall total column is added to each detail row:

```
SELECT e.EmployeeKey, e.LastName,
 fr.SalesAmount,
 (SELECT SUM(fr1.SalesAmount)
  FROM dbo.FactResellerSales AS fr1
  WHERE fr1.EmployeeKey = e.EmployeeKey)
  AS TotalPerEmployee,
 frt.GrandTotal
FROM (dbo.DimEmployee AS e
 INNER JOIN dbo.FactResellerSales AS fr
 ON e.EmployeeKey = fr.EmployeeKey)
 CROSS JOIN
  (SELECT SUM(fr2.SalesAmount) AS GrandTotal
   FROM dbo.FactResellerSales AS fr2) AS frt
ORDER BY e.EmployeeKey;
```

Here is the abbreviated output of the previous query:

```
EmployeeKey LastName   SalesAmount   TotelPerEmployee GrandTotal
----------- ---------- ------------- ---------------- -------------
272         Jiang      1619.52       1092123.8562     80450596.9823
272         Jiang      1445.1898     1092123.8562     80450596.9823
272         Jiang      714.7043      1092123.8562     80450596.9823
```

In the previous example code, the correlated subquery in the SELECT clause has to logically execute once per row of the outer query. The query was partially optimized by moving the self-contained subquery for the overall total in the FROM clause, where it logically executes only once. Although SQL Server can optimize correlated subqueries and convert them to joins, there exists a much better and more efficient way to achieve the same result as the previous query returned. You can do this by using the window functions.

Window functions

The following query uses the SUM window aggregate function to calculate the total over each employee and the overall total. The OVER clause defines the partitions, or the windows of the calculation. The first calculation is partitioned over each employee, meaning that the total quantity per employee is reset to zero for each new employee. The second calculation uses an OVER clause without specifying partitions, meaning the calculation is done over all input rowsets. This query produces exactly the same result as the previous one:

```
SELECT e.EmployeeKey, e.LastName,
 fr.SalesAmount,
 SUM(fr.SalesAmount) OVER(PARTITION BY e.EmployeeKey)
  AS TotalPerEmployee,
 SUM(fr.SalesAmount) OVER()
 AS GrandTotal
FROM dbo.DimEmployee AS e
 INNER JOIN dbo.FactResellerSales AS fr
  ON e.EmployeeKey = fr.EmployeeKey
ORDER BY e.EmployeeKey;
```

Now assume that you need to calculate some statistics of the totals of the employees' orders. You need to calculate the running total amount for employees, and the moving average of this total over the last three employees, ordered by the employee key. This means you need to calculate the totals over employees in advance, and then use aggregate functions on these aggregates. You could do aggregations over employees in advance in a derived table. However, there is another way to achieve this. You can define the derived table in advance, in the WITH clause of the SELECT statement. This subquery is called a **common table expression**, or **CTE**.

Common table expressions

CTEs are more readable than derived tables and might be also more efficient. You could use the result of the same CTE multiple times in the outer query. If you use derived tables, you need to define them multiple times if you want to use them multiple times in the outer query. The following query shows the usage of CTE to calculate the total amount for all employees and then just shows the results in the outer query:

```
WITH EmpTotalCTE AS
(
SELECT e.EmployeeKey,
 MIN(e.LastName) AS LastName,
 SUM(fr.SalesAmount) AS TotalPerEmployee
FROM dbo.DimEmployee AS e
 INNER JOIN dbo.FactResellerSales AS fr
  ON e.EmployeeKey = fr.EmployeeKey
GROUP BY e.EmployeeKey
)
SELECT EmployeeKey, LastName,
 TotalPerEmployee
FROM EmpTotalCTE
ORDER BY EmployeeKey;
```

The query returns 17 rows, one for each employee, with the total sales amount for this employee. Now let's add the running total and the moving average in the outer query:

```
WITH EmpTotalCTE AS
(
SELECT e.EmployeeKey,
 MIN(e.LastName) AS LastName,
 SUM(fr.SalesAmount) AS TotalPerEmployee
FROM dbo.DimEmployee AS e
 INNER JOIN dbo.FactResellerSales AS fr
  ON e.EmployeeKey = fr.EmployeeKey
GROUP BY e.EmployeeKey
)
SELECT EmployeeKey, LastName,
 TotalPerEmployee,
 SUM(TotalPerEmployee)
  OVER(ORDER BY EmploYeeKey
       ROWS BETWEEN UNBOUNDED PRECEDING
                AND CURRENT ROW)
  AS RunningTotal,
 AVG(TotalPerEmployee)
  OVER(ORDER BY EmploYeeKey
```

```
        ROWS BETWEEN 2 PRECEDING
                    AND CURRENT ROW)
  AS MovingAverage
FROM EmpTotalCTE
ORDER BY EmployeeKey;
```

Here are the partial results with the first five and last two rows:

```
EmployeeKey LastName  TotelPerEmployee RunningTotal   MovingAverage
----------- --------- ---------------- -------------- -------------
272         Jiang     1092123.8562     1092123.8562   1092123.8562
281         Blythe    9293903.0055     10386026.8617  5193013.4308
282         Mitchell  10367007.4286    20753034.2903  6917678.0967
283         Carson    10065803.5429    30818837.8332  9908904.659
284         Vargas    3609447.2163     34428285.0495  8014086.0626
...
295         Valdez    1790640.2311     79028786.0571  1425236.791
296         Tsoflias  1421810.9252     80450596.9823  1128325.2026
```

Note that the running total for the last employee, sorted by the employee key, is the grand total. You can also check whether the running total and moving average are calculated correctly.

In the previous query, you can see that in the OVER() clause, I defined the frame of the calculation of the running total and the moving average for each row. For the running total, the frame is all rows from the first row in the window to the current row, and for the moving average, it is the last three rows, including the current row.

You can use many other functions for window calculations. For example, you can use the ranking functions, such as ROW_NUMBER(), to calculate some rank in the window or in the overall rowset. However, rank can be defined only over some order of the calculation. You can specify the order of the calculation in the ORDER BY sub-clause inside the OVER clause. Please note that this ORDER BY clause defines only the logical order of the calculation, and not the order of the rows returned. A standalone, outer ORDER BY at the end of the query defines the order of the result.

The following query calculates a sequential number, the row number of each row in the output, for each detail row of the input rowset. The row number is calculated once in partitions for each employee and defines the row number or the position of every single reseller for each employee, ordered by the sales amount, in descending order:

```
WITH EmpResTotalCTE AS
(
SELECT e.EmployeeKey, r.ResellerKey,
 MIN(e.LastName) AS LastName,
 MIN(r.ResellerName) AS ResellerName,
```

```
    SUM(fr.SalesAmount) AS EmpResTotal
FROM dbo.DimEmployee AS e
  INNER JOIN dbo.FactResellerSales AS fr
   ON e.EmployeeKey = fr.EmployeeKey
  INNER JOIN dbo.DimReseller AS r
   ON r.ResellerKey = fr.ResellerKey
GROUP BY e.EmployeeKey, r.ResellerKey
)
SELECT EmployeeKey, LastName,
 ResellerName, EmpResTotal,
 ROW_NUMBER()
  OVER(PARTITION BY EmployeeKey ORDER BY EmpResTotal DESC)
  AS PositionByEmployee
FROM EmpResTotalCTE
ORDER BY EmployeeKey, EmpResTotal DESC;
```

Here are the partial results:

```
EmployeeKey LastName  ResellerName        EmpResTotal   PositionByEmployee
----------- --------  --------------      -----------   ------------------
272         Jiang     Thorough Parts      198993.3507   1
272         Jiang     Sheet Metal         138046.3212   2
272         Jiang     Vigorous Exercise   125422.2079   3
272         Jiang     Sales and Supply    79994.1743    4
...
281         Blythe    Totes & Baskets     463030.757    1
281         Blythe    First Bike          437319.784    2
281         Blythe    Modular Cycle       389208.6639   3
281         Blythe    Fitness Toy Store   375100.3084   4
...
296         Tsoflias  Eastside Cycle      2223.7009     30
296         Tsoflias  Twin Cycles         1336.23       31
296         Tsoflias  Kids and Adults     753.768       32
296         Tsoflias  Major Bicycle       200.052       33
```

In the abbreviated results shown previously, each sales amount total for each reseller and employee combination is unique. That's why all of the row numbers are in the right position – 1 is before 2, which is before 3, and so on. Now imagine that the second and the third reseller (Sheet Metal and Vigorous Exercise) for the first employee (Jiang) would have the same total, for example 138,046.3212. Then you could get the wrong order of row numbers in the results, as shown here:

```
EmployeeKey LastName  ResellerName     EmpResTotal   PositionByEmployee
----------- --------  --------------   -----------   ------------------
272         Jiang     Thorough Parts   198993.3507   1
```

```
272          Jiang      Vigorous Exercise 138046.3212  3
272          Jiang      Sheet Metal       138046.3212  2
272          Jiang      Sales and Supply  79994.1743   4
```

The order of the result is defined over the sales total, and not over the row number. You can't know in advance which row will get which row number when the order of the calculation is not defined in unique values.

Finding top n rows and using the APPLY operator

Let's find the top-6 sales based on the sales amount. You can do this by using the OFFSET...FETCH clause after the ORDER BY clause:

```
SELECT SalesOrderNumber,
 SalesOrderLineNumber,
 SalesAmount
FROM dbo.FactResellerSales
ORDER BY SalesAmount DESC
OFFSET 0 ROWS FETCH NEXT 6 ROWS ONLY;
```

Here are the results:

```
SalesOrderNumber   SalesOrderLineNumber  SalesAmount
-----------------  --------------------  -----------
SO55282            39                    27893.619
SO43884            17                    27055.7604
SO51131            12                    26159.2081
SO43875            12                    24938.4761
SO57054            26                    23667.8549
SO43875            10                    23190.6518
```

The question that arises is whether order SO43875, line number 10, is the only sale with the sales amount equal to 23190.6518. You could try to execute the previous query again, but with limiting the output to the first seven rows, then eight rows, and so on. SQL Server offers another possibility, the TOP clause. You can specify TOP n WITH TIES, meaning you can get all of the rows with ties on the last value in the output. However, this way, you don't know the number of the rows in the output in advance. The following query shows this approach:

```
SELECT TOP 6 WITH TIES
 SalesOrderNumber, SalesOrderLineNumber,
 SalesAmount
FROM dbo.FactResellerSales
ORDER BY SalesAmount DESC;
```

In the results of the last query, you get seven rows:

```
SalesOrderNumber   SalesOrderLineNumber  SalesAmount
------------------ --------------------- -----------
SO55282            39                    27893.619
SO43884            17                    27055.7604
SO51131            12                    26159.2081
SO43875            12                    24938.4761
SO57054            26                    23667.8549
SO44795            18                    23190.6518
SO43875            10                    23190.6518
```

The next task is to get the top three resellers by amount for a specific employee. Here is the query that returns the top four resellers for the employee with the employee key equal to 272:

```
SELECT TOP 3
  fr.EmployeeKey, fr.ResellerKey,
  SUM(fr.SalesAmount) AS EmpResTotal
FROM dbo.FactResellerSales AS fr
WHERE fr.EmployeeKey = 272
GROUP BY fr.EmployeeKey, fr.ResellerKey
ORDER BY EmpResTotal DESC;
```

You need to perform the calculation for each employee. The APPLY Transact-SQL operator comes in handy here. You use it in the FROM clause. You apply, or execute, a table expression defined on the right side of the operator once for each row of the input rowset from the left side of the operator. There are two flavors of this operator. The CROSS APPLY version filters out the rows from the left rowset if the tabular expression on the right side does not return any row. The OUTER APPLY version preserves the row from the left side, even is the tabular expression on the right side does not return any row, similar to LEFT OUTER JOIN. Of course, columns for the preserved rows do not have known values from the right-side tabular expression. The following query uses the CROSS APPLY operator to calculate top three resellers by amount for each employee that actually does have some sales:

```
SELECT e.EmployeeKey, e.LastName,
  fr1.ResellerKey, fr1.EmpResTotal
FROM dbo.DimEmployee AS e
  CROSS APPLY
  (SELECT TOP 3
    fr.EmployeeKey, fr.ResellerKey,
    SUM(fr.SalesAmount) AS EmpResTotal
  FROM dbo.FactResellerSales AS fr
```

```
   WHERE fr.EmployeeKey = e.EmployeeKey
   GROUP BY fr.EmployeeKey, fr.ResellerKey
   ORDER BY EmpResTotal DESC) AS fr1
ORDER BY e.EmployeeKey, fr1.EmpResTotal DESC;
```

The query returns 51 rows. You can see the abbreviated results here:

```
EmployeeKey LastName    ResellerKey EmpResTotal
----------- ----------  ----------- -----------
272         Jiang       433         198993.3507
272         Jiang       436         138046.3212
272         Jiang       678         125422.2079
281         Blythe      328         463030.757
281         Blythe      670         437319.784
281         Blythe      4           389208.6639
...
296         Tsoflias    573         163398.0205
296         Tsoflias    87          148996.5063
296         Tsoflias    393         145407.7395
```

Since this was the last query in this chapter, you can clean up your demo database with the following code:

```
DROP TABLE dbo.EmpFUll;
GO
```

That's it for T-SQL for now. You will use this knowledge a lot in the forthcoming chapters for concrete data science tasks.

Summary

In this chapter, you were given a quick introduction to the mighty T-SQL SELECT statement. You are ready to query the data you have stored in a SQL Server database. However, T-SQL is a language that is specialized to work with data, to query and modify it. It logically operates on a whole dataset at once. When operating on a whole set of data, T-SQL is extremely efficient. However, it is not very efficient for advanced mathematical operations inside a single row and between rows in a row-by-row manner. This is not very appropriate for the data science tasks, where you often need to perform such advanced mathematical analyses. Therefore, we need another language. In the next chapter, you will learn about the first option, the R language.

Introducing R 2

When you talk about statistics, data mining, and machine learning, many people, especially those working in academic areas, think about R. R is the language that the engine that executes the code. You can use different R distributions, or versions of R engines and development tools; however, there is only one basic R language. Of course, to use it, you need to learn how to program in this language.

Statistics, data mining, and machine learning terms are very similar. You won't make a big mistake if you use them as synonyms. Statistics is the science of analyzing data collections, expressing the relationships as mathematical functions, and presenting and interpreting the results. In statistics, you usually work with sample data, or **samples**, because the population data, or the **census**, is not available to you. Data-mining analysis techniques are often derived from statistics, but also from artificial intelligence, biology, and other scientific areas. You use these techniques, or algorithms, on your data with the purpose of discovering hidden **patterns** and **rules**. You use those patterns and rules for **predictions**. Machine learning means doing some programming to apply similar algorithms to your data to solve a given problem automatically. As you can see from the previous sentences, the three definitions overlap. You might define small differences between them depending on the users of the results: statistics is typically used by scientists, data mining is aimed at business people, and machine learning frequently tries to improve automatic work or machines. As mentioned, all three areas of this applied math use many common algorithms, so there is a lot of overlap among them.

This chapter will cover the following points:

- Obtaining R
- Tools for developing R code
- R basics

Obtaining R

R is open source and free. R distribution is maintained by **Comprehensive R Archive Network (CRAN)** site at `https://cran.r-project.org/`. From this site, you can download the R engine for multiple platforms, including Windows, Linux, and macOS X. Besides CRAN, Microsoft also gives a free R download on the **Microsoft R Application Network (MRAN)** site at `https://mran.revolutionanalytics.com/`, which is where you can get Microsoft R Open. This is the open source R from Microsoft, which is the core R with additional Microsoft libraries. If you install Visual Studio 2017, you can also get Microsoft R Open—actually, you get what's called Microsoft R Client, which I will introduce in a minute.

After you install R, you can start working by using the R console client tool. With this tool, you can write code line by line. You can use also any of a plethora of additional tools. The most widely-used free tool is RStudio IDE. There are payable and free versions of this tool. You can download it from the RStudio company site at `https://www.rstudio.com/`.

Microsoft created **R Tools for Visual Studio (RTVS)** for developers that are used to Microsoft tools, and an environment for development. RTVS are available in **Visual Studio (VS)** 2015 as a free download, and are already included in VS 2017. You don't need to pay for Visual Studio if you are not a professional developer. You can use the free Community edition to develop R (and also Python) code. Of course, you get additional features by buying the Professional or even the Enterprise edition. All VS editions are available for download from the VS download site at `https://www.visualstudio.com/downloads/`.

When installing VS 2017 for coding in R or Python, you need to select the **Python development** workload, and then **Data science and analytical applications**. You can see this selection in the following screenshot. With this selection, you install Python language templates, which include the data science templates, and R Tools for Visual Studio:

Figure 2.1: Visual Studio 2017 setup for data science

As mentioned, by installing VS 2017 for data science applications, you get the Microsoft R engine, called Microsoft R Client. You also get a free Python engine. I will deal more with Python in `Chapter 3`, *Getting Familiar with Python*. Microsoft R Client is an enhanced version of Microsoft R Open, which ships with additional scalable Microsoft R libraries, such as `RevoScaleR` and `MicrosoftML`. Readers of this book will probably want to perform the data science with SQL Server. Therefore, I would strongly suggest you use the MS R Client. This way, at development and testing time, you can use in your code all of the libraries available in the MS ML Services, the server-side R, and Python engine, which is a standalone product or part of SQL Server installation, as you learned in `Chapter 1`, *Writing Queries with T-SQL*.

Your first line R of code in R

R engine is an interpreter. Therefore, R is an interpreted language. In addition, R is a case-sensitive and functional language. Instead of typing commands, you call functions to perform an action. For example, to quit an R session, you need to call the `q()` function. You should extensively comment your code. A comment starts with a hash mark (#); you can use the comment anywhere in the line of code.

Any code after the start of the comment does not execute. A semicolon (`;`) is a command delimiter if you write more than one command in a single line. A new line is the command delimiter as well. The following code example shows a comment, displays my R version, and lists the authors and other contributors to the language using the `contributors()` function:

```
# R version and contributors
R.version.string
contributors()
```

Here, I am only showing the version I am currently using. Note that by the time you read this book, you might already have a newer version:

```
"R version 3.3.2 (2016-10-31)"
```

If you are using VS 2017 to develop R code, you start by creating a new R project. You get an empty R Script; if you are used to RStudio IDE, this R Script environment will be familiar to you. The top-left window is where you write the R code. When you have the cursor in a line of code and press the *Ctrl* and *Enter* keys at the same time, the R engine executes this line of code. You can see the result in the console window at the bottom of the screen. In this console window, you can also write the commands directly, just like in the basic R console client tool mentioned earlier, and then execute them line by line.

When developing in R, help is always available to you. You start with the `help()` function, you start the help and open the **Help** window (by default at the bottom-right of the screen). The `help.start()` function guides you to the free R documentation. In the R environment you are using, there are some global options set. These options affect the way in which the R engine executes the computations and displays the results. You can use the `help("options")` function to examine these options. Every specific function also has help associated with it.

You can call the help function with a parameter to get help about the function, such as `help("exp")` to get help with the exponential function. Instead of writing the full `help()` function name, you can use the question mark as the shortcut. With `?"exp"`, you also display help for the exponential function. Besides help, you can also get code examples for calling a function. Use `example("exp")` to get code examples for the exponential function. With `help.search("topic")` or `??"topic"`, you search help for a specific topic. You can extend the search to the online documentation with `RSiteSearch("topic")`. The following code examples show all of these help options:

```
help()            # Getting help on help
help.start()      # General help
help("options")   # Help about global options
help("exp")       # Help on the function exp()
?"exp"            # Help on the function exp()
example("exp")    # Examples for the function exp()
help.search("constants")   # Search
??"constants"              # Search
RSiteSearch("exp")         # Online search
```

You can see the help in the **Help** window at the right side of the screen, right below the **Solution Explorer**. For the last command in the previous code block, the online search command, your default web browser should open at the appropriate site with the help for the `exp()` function.

There is also the very useful `demo()` function. You use this function to run demo scripts, which show you the capabilities of the function or R environment you are investigating. To check the R graphic capabilities, you can use the following code:

```
demo("graphics")
```

When you execute this code, a graphic widow opens. However, before that, you need to move the cursor in the **Console** pane and then execute the pieces of demo code, graph by graph, by hitting the *Enter* key. I copied one part of the demo code that creates an exemplary pie chart:

```
pie.sales <- c(0.12, 0.3, 0.26, 0.16, 0.04, 0.12)
names(pie.sales) <- c("Blueberry", "Cherry", "Apple",
                      "Boston Cream", "Other", "Vanilla Cream")
pie(pie.sales,
    col = c("purple", "violetred1", "green3", "cornsilk", "cyan", "white"))
title(main = "January Pie Sales", cex.main = 1.8, font.main = 1)
title(xlab = "(Don't try this at home kids)", cex.lab = 0.8, font.lab = 3)
```

The following diagram shows the results of the demo code:

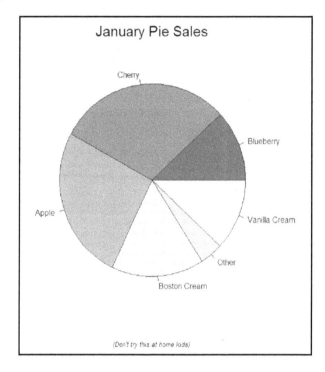

Figure 2.2: Demo pie chart

When you use the open R editions, you create all of the objects in memory. This is a limitation for the scalability. The ML Services engine can spill data to disk as well. For development, the Microsoft R Client is usually sufficient. Each session (each R script you are developing and executing) has its own **workspace**. You don't need to lose these objects when you finish a session by closing the R script window or by exiting VS; you can save the objects from memory (the workspace) to disk in a `.RData` file. you can load the object by loading that file in the next session. The workspace is saved in a default folder. You can check the default working folder with the `getwd()` function call.

You can change the default folder with the `setwd(dir)` function, where the `dir` parameter is the new folder, or the new directory. You can always check the objects in memory, or in the current workspace, by calling the `objects()` or `ls()` function.

With the `rm(objectname)` function, you can always remove an object from memory. Besides showing graphs interactively, you can save the images in different graphical formats. You can even save a single object to a specific file. The following code example shows how to divert the output to a file with the `sink()` command:

```
sink("C:\\DataScienceSQLServer\\Chapter02.txt")
getwd()
sink()
```

The second `sink()` call redirects the output to the console. You can check the content of the file by yourself.

Learning the basics of the R language

Now let's write some code that actually executes something:

```
1 + 2
2 + 5 * 4
3 ^ 4
sqrt(81)
pi
```

This code first evaluates three mathematical expressions using the basic operators. As you might expect, R evaluates the expressions using the mathematical operator precedence. The code calls the `sqrt()` function to calculate and checks the value of the constant for the number pi (π). The base R installation, or the base package, has many built-in constants. You can search the help for all pages that mention constants with `??"constants"`.

There are many ways to generate **sequences** of numbers, as you can see from the following code:

```
rep(1, 5)
4:8
seq(4, 8)
seq(4, 20, by = 3)
```

The first command replicates the number 1 five times with the help of the `rep()` function. You can generate a sequence of numbers with the help of the colon operator (`:`), as you can see from the second line. In the third line, I am using the `seq()` function for the same task. This function has more possibilities, as the fourth line of the code shows. You can define an increment as the third parameter, besides the lower and the upper bound, when you call this function.

Here are the generated sequences:

```
[1] 1 1 1 1 1
[1] 4 5 6 7 8
[1] 4 5 6 7 8
[1] 4 7 10 13 16 19
```

You can store the values in **variables**. Storing a value in a variable means assigning a variable a value; you do that with an **assignment operator**. There are multiple assignment operators in R. The most popular is the left assignment operator (<-); you write the variable name on the left side and the value on the right side of the operator. You can reverse the order of the variable and the value with the right assignment operator (->). The equals (=) operator is used in the same way as the left assignment operator. The following code assigns the numbers 2, 3, and 4 to 3 variables and then does some calculations using these three variables:

```
x <- 2
y <- 3
z <- 4
x + y * z
```

You can execute the code to check that the result is 14. As I mentioned, the R language is case sensitive. Therefore, you get an error if you execute the following line of code. The X, Y, and Z variable names written with capital letters are not defined:

```
X + Y + Z
```

A variable or an object name can include a dot. This allows you to organize your objects into virtual namespaces, similar to .NET languages, as you can see in the following example. However, note that the namespaces are not real. There is no hierarchy; a dot is just a part of the name, and you could replace it with an underscore, if you prefer this character:

```
This.Year <- 2018
This.Year
```

R also includes **logical operators**. Note that the equals operator is the assignment operator; to test the equality, you need to use the double equals (==) operator. Logical operators include the inequality operators: <, <=, >, >=, and !=. You can combine two or more logical expressions with the logical AND (&) and the logical OR (|) operators. The following code shows you how to use the equals operator the same way as the previous code used the left assignment operator, and then how to perform some logical tests:

```
# Equals as an assignment operator
x = 2
```

```
y = 3
z = 4
x + y * z
# Boolean equality test
x <- 2
x == 2
```

The results of the code are as follows:

```
[1] 14
[1] TRUE
```

In R, every variable is actually an **object**. You can treat a scalar variable as a vector of length one. A real vector is a one-dimensional array of scalars of the same type. The data type is also called the **mode** in R. Basic types include numeric, character, logical, complex (imaginary numbers), and raw (bytes). You define a vector with the combine function: `c()`. The following code shows you the various ways you can create a vector in R. Besides the assignment operators you are already familiar with, the example also uses the `assign()` function. The value of the variable used earlier in the code is overwritten with the new value:

```
x <- c(2, 0, 0, 4)
assign("y", c(1, 9, 9, 9))
c(5, 4, 3, 2) -> z
q = c(1, 2, 3, 4)
```

You use operators on vectors just as you would use them on scalar values. The operators work element by element. Here are some mathematical operations on the x vector defined in the previous code:

```
x + y
x * 4
sqrt(x)
```

Here are the results of these mathematical operations:

```
[1]  3   9   9 13
[1]  8   0   0 16
[1] 1.414214 0.000000 0.000000 2.00000
```

Instead of using the whole vector, you can operate on a selected element or selected elements of a vector only. Every element has numerical index values assigned to it. The index starts at 1. The following code shows how you can refer to the index to operate on specific elements only:

```
x <- c(2, 0, 0, 4)
x[1]             # Selects the first element
```

```
x[-1]           # Excludes the first element
x[1] <- 3       # Assigns a value to the first element
x               # Show the vector
x[-1] = 5       # Assigns a value to all other elements
x               # Show the vector
```

From the comments, you can see what the code does to the vector and its elements. The results are as follows:

```
[1] 2
[1] 0 0 4
[1] 3 0 0 4
[1] 3 5 5 5
```

The logical operators on vectors work element by element as well, as you can see from the following code:

```
y <- c(1, 9, 9, 9)
y < 8           # Compares each element, returns result as vector
y[4] = 1        # Assigns a value to the first element
y < 8           # Compares each element, returns result as vector
y[y < 8] = 2    # Edits elements marked as TRUE in index vector
y               # Shows the vector
```

Again, you can see from the comments what the code does. Here are the results:

```
[1]   TRUE FALSE FALSE FALSE
[1]   TRUE FALSE FALSE  TRUE
[1]   2 9 9 2
```

Scalars and vectors are the most basic data structures. There are many more advanced data structures, which I will introduce in the later of this chapter. But, before that, let me introduce the R packages.

 Although the capabilities of the core R engine are already very extensive, the real power of R comes with thousands of additional packages.

You can easily download and install packages. A package typically adds some functions to core R. Some packages also bring demo data. The number of available packages is enormous and still growing. There is probably no other language with so many additional data science modules and contributors that write those modules as R (the total number of modules is higher in some languages, such as Python; however, the number of modules intended for data science is the strength of R).

In the summer of 2018, as I am writing this chapter, the number of available packages is already more than 12,000. When you install the core engine, you get a small set of widely-used, or base, packages.

You can use the `installed.packages()` function to check which packages are already installed in your library. The library is stored and available in a folder; you can get this folder name with the `.libPaths()` function (note the dot in the name). With the `library()` function, you can list the packages in your library. When you call this function, a new R package-manager window opens. You can see the installed, available, and loaded packages in this window. Here is the example code showing the three functions I just mentioned:

```
installed.packages()
.libPaths()
library()
```

Use `install.packages("packagename")` to install a new package. When you execute it, it searches the CRAN sites for the package, downloads it, unzips it, and installs it. You need a web connection to download a package directly. This approach is good for development and testing, but not for production servers. You can also download packages separately, and then install them from a local file.

You load an installed package to memory with the `library(packagename)` command. As you already know, in R, help is always nearby. Use the `help(package ="packagename")` command to get help for a specific package. Let's say you want to read the data from a SQL Server database. For this task, you need the RODBC package. Use the following code to install it, load it, and get help on it:

```
install.packages("RODBC")
library(RODBC)
help(package = "RODBC")
```

Now you can read the data from SQL Server. But you need to perform some other tasks to read the data successfully. Your R code needs access to SQL Server and must have permission to read the data. In SQL Server, you need to create a **login** and a **database user** for the R session. Then you need to **authorize** this user to read the data by giving it appropriate **permissions**. You also must have an ODBC **data source name** (**DSN**) that points to the database where your data is stored. In SQL Server Management Studio, you can use the GUI for these tasks. You have to connect to your SQL Server, and then in **Object Explorer**, expand the **Security** folder. Right-click the **Logins** subfolder. Create a new login. Map this login to a database user in the AdventureWorksDW2017 demo database. You can add this user to the **db_datareader** role in the same window to authorize this user to read the data. In my example, my SQL Server login is called RUser.

The password for this login is Pa$$w0rd. I created a database user with the same name, mapped it to this login, and added the database user to the **db_datareader** role, as the following screenshot shows:

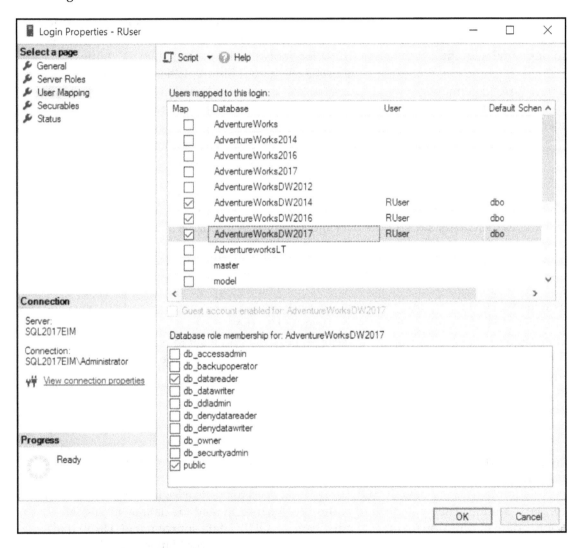

Figure 2.3: Generating the RUser login and database user

Then I run the ODBC Data Sources tool. With this tool, I created a system DSN called AWDW. I configured the DSN to connect to my local SQL Server with the RUser SQL Server login I just created, and change the context to the `AdventureWorksDW2017` database. When you finish these steps, you can execute the following code to read the data from the `dbo.vTargetMail` view from the `AdventureWorksDW2017` demo database:

```
con <- odbcConnect("AWDW", uid = "RUser", pwd = "Pa$$w0rd")
sqlQuery(con,
        "SELECT CustomerKey,
            EnglishEducation AS Education,
            Age, NumberCarsOwned, BikeBuyer
        FROM dbo.vTargetMail;")
close(con)
```

If you execute the code, you should get 18,484 rows of output in the Console pane. You can see the first four rows here:

```
    CustomerKey         Education Age NumberCarsOwned BikeBuyer
1         11000         Bachelors  31               0         1
2         11001         Bachelors  27               1         1
3         11002         Bachelors  32               1         1
4         11003         Bachelors  29               1         1
```

If you prefer not to create an ODBC DSN, you can use an ad hoc connection from R, as the following code shows:

```
con <- odbcDriverConnect('driver={SQL Server};server=SQL2017EIM;
  database=AdventureWorksDW2017;uid=RUser;pwd=Pa$$w0rd')
```

Using R data structures

As promised, I am now introducing the most important **data structures** in R. When you analyze the data, you analyze a **dataset**. A dataset looks like a SQL Server table: you can observe rows and columns. However, this is not a table in the relational sense, as defined in the Relational Model, which SQL Server follows. The order of rows and columns is not defined in a table that conforms to the Relational Model. However, in R, positions of cells as crossings of rows and columns are known. This is more like a matrix in mathematics.

In the R dataset, rows are also called **cases** or **observations**. You analyze the cases by using the values in their columns, also called **variables** or **attributes** of the cases.

I will introduce the following data structures in this section:

- Matrices and arrays
- Factors
- Lists
- Data frames

A **matrix** is a two-dimensional array. All of the values of a matrix must have the same mode – you can have integers only, or strings only, and so on. Use the `matrix()` function to generate a matrix from a vector. You can assign labels to columns and rows. When you create a matrix from a vector, you define whether you generate it by rows or by columns (default). You will quickly understand the difference if you execute the following demo code:

```
x = c(1, 2, 3, 4, 5, 6); x
Y = array(x, dim = c(2, 3)); Y
Z = matrix(x, 2, 3, byrow = F); Z
U = matrix(x, 2, 3, byrow = T); U
```

Please note that there are two commands in each line, separated by a semicolon. Also note that I used the `array()` function in the second line to generate the same matrix that the third line does, generating the matrix by columns. The last command generates a matrix by rows. Here is the output of the previous code:

```
[1] 1 2 3 4 5 6
     [,1] [,2] [,3]
[1,]    1    3    5
[2,]    2    4    6
     [,1] [,2] [,3]
[1,]    1    3    5
[2,]    2    4    6
     [,1] [,2] [,3]
[1,]    1    2    3
[2,]    4    5    6
```

The following code shows how to define explicit names for rows and columns:

```
rnames = c("rrr1", "rrr2")
cnames = c("ccc1", "ccc2", "ccc3")
V = matrix(x, 2, 3, byrow = T,
    dimnames = list(rnames, cnames))
V
```

Here is the result:

```
      ccc1 ccc2 ccc3
rrr1    1    2    3
rrr2    4    5    6
```

You can refer to the elements of a matrix by index positions or by names, if you defined the names. The following code shows you some options. Note that you always refer to the row and column indexes; however, when you skip an explicit index value, this means all of the elements for that index. For example, the first line of code selects the first row, all columns. The third line selects all rows, but the second and third column only:

```
U[1,]
U[1, c(2, 3)]
U[, c(2, 3)]
V[, c("ccc2", "ccc3")]
```

The results are as follows:

```
[1] 1 2 3
[1] 2 3
      [,1] [,2]
[1,]    2    3
[2,]    5    6
      ccc2 ccc3
Row1    2    3
Row2    5    6
```

You saw that I generated a matrix with the `array()` function as well. An **array** is a generalized, multi-dimensional matrix. The `array()` function, similar to the `matrix()` function, accepts a vector of values as the first input parameter. The second parameter is a vector where you define the number of dimensions with the number of elements in this vector, and the number of elements in each dimension with the values in this vector. You can also pass a list of vectors for the names of the dimensions' elements. An array is filled by columns, then by rows, then by the third dimension (pages), and so on. The following code shows how to create an array:

```
rnames = c("rrr1", "rrr2")
cnames = c("ccc1", "ccc2", "ccc3")
pnames = c("ppp1", "ppp2", "ppp3")
Y = array(1:18, dim = c(2, 3, 3),
  dimnames = list(rnames, cnames, pnames))
Y
```

Multidimensional arrays are not useful for typical data science analyses. Therefore, I will not use them anymore in this book. Of course, you can use them for your own purposes, such as for algebraic operations.

Before introducing the data frame, I need to discuss how the variables store their values. A variable is **discrete** when every value is taken from a limited pool of possible values. A variable is **continuous** if the pool of possible values is not limited. Discrete values can be **nominal**, or **categorical**, where they represent labels only, without any specific order, or **ordinal**, where a logical ordering of the values makes sense. In R, discrete variables are called **factors**. **Levels** of a factor are the distinct values that make the pool of possible values. You define factors from vectors of values with the `factor()` function. Many statistics, data mining, and machine learning algorithms treat discrete and continuous variables differently. Therefore, you need to define the factors properly in advance, before analyzing them. Here are some examples of defining the factors:

```
x = c("good", "moderate", "good", "bad", "bad", "good")
y = factor(x); y
z = factor(x, order = TRUE); z
w = factor(x, order = TRUE,
          levels = c("bad", "moderate", "good")); w
```

The previous code produces the following result:

```
[1] good      moderate good      bad      bad      good
Levels: bad good moderate
[1] good      moderate good      bad      bad      good
Levels: bad < good < moderate
[1] good      moderate good      bad      bad      good
Levels: bad < moderate < good
```

You can see how R recognized distinct levels when I defined that the vector represents a factor. You can also see how R sorted the levels alphabetically by default, when in the third line of the previous code I defined the factor as an ordinal variable. In the last command, I finally defined the correct order for the factor.

Lists are complex data structures. Lists can include any other data structure, including another list. Typically, you analyze a list. However, you need to know about them because some functions return complex results packed in a list, and some functions accept lists as parameters. You create lists with the `list()` function. As lists are also ordered, you can refer to the objects in a list by position. You need to enclose the index number in double brackets. If an element is a vector or a matrix, you can use the index position(s) of the elements of this vector in a matrix, enclosed in single brackets. Here is an example of using a list:

```
L = list(name1 = "ABC", name2 = "DEF",
```

```
                 no.children = 2, children.ages = c(3, 6))
L
L[[1]]
L[[4]]
L[[4]][2]
```

This example code for working with lists returns the following result:

```
$name1
[1] "ABC"
$name2
[1] "DEF"
$no.children
[1] 2
$children.ages
[1] 3 6
[1] "ABC"
[1] 3 6
[1] 6
```

The most important data structure for any data science analysis is a **data frame**. Data frames are generalized two-dimensional matrices where each variable can have a different mode, or a different data type. Of course, all the values of a variable must be of the same data type. This is very similar to SQL Server tables. But data frames are matrices, so you can use the positional access to refer to the values of a data frame. You can create a data frame from multiple vectors of different modes with the data.frame() function. All of the vectors must be of the same length and must have the same number of elements. Here is an example:

```
CategoryId = c(1, 2, 3, 4)
CategoryName = c("Bikes", "Components", "Clothing", "Accessories")
ProductCategories = data.frame(CategoryId, CategoryName)
ProductCategories
```

The result is as follows:

```
  CategoryId CategoryName
1          1        Bikes
2          2   Components
3          3     Clothing
4          4  Accessories
```

In an earlier example in this chapter, I read the data from a view in a SQL Server database. I showed the data in the console window directly. This was not very useful for further analysis. Most of the time, what you want is to store the data you read in a data frame. The dataset you analyze is your data frame. SQL Server is definitely not the only source of data you can use. You read the data from many other sources, including text files and Excel. The following code retrieves the data from the `dbo.vtargetMail` view from the `AdventureWorksDW2017` demo database in a data frame, and then displays the first five columns for the first five rows of the data frame:

```
con <- odbcConnect("AWDW", uid = "RUser", pwd = "Pa$$w0rd")
TM <-
sqlQuery(con,
         "SELECT CustomerKey,
            EnglishEducation AS Education,
            Age, NumberCarsOwned, BikeBuyer
          FROM dbo.vTargetMail;")
close(con)
TM[1:5, 1:5]
```

Here is the content of these first five rows of the data frame:

```
  CustomerKey Education Age NumberCarsOwned BikeBuyer
1       11000 Bachelors  31               0         1
2       11001 Bachelors  27               1         1
3       11002 Bachelors  32               1         1
4       11003 Bachelors  29               1         1
5       11004 Bachelors  23               4         1
```

You can also see the complete data frame in a separate window that opens after you execute the following command:

```
View(TM)
```

As you have just seen, you can retrieve the data from a data frame by using positional indices, as in matrices. You can also use column names. However, the most common notation is using the data frame name and column name, separated by the dollar ($) sign, such as TM$Education. The following code uses the R `table()` function to produce a cross-tabulation of NumberCarsOwned and BikeBuyer:

```
table(TM$NumberCarsOwned, TM$BikeBuyer)
```

Here is the last result in this chapter:

```
        0    1
0  1551  2687
1  2187  2696
2  3868  2589
3   951   694
4   795   466
```

This data frame concludes our short introduction to R data structures.

Summary

This chapter gave you an overview of the R language. You learned the basics, including how to write R expressions and create variables. The chapter introduced the data structures in R, with an emphasis on the most important one, the data frame. You saw how to read the data from SQL Server, store it in a data frame, and then retrieve it from the data frame. In `Chapter 3`, *Getting Familiar with Python*, before doing some additional manipulation of the data in a data frame to prepare it for further analysis, we will have a short introduction to the Python language.

3
Getting Familiar with Python

Python is a general-purpose high-level interpreted language. Because it is a general-purpose language, it is probably even more popular than R or T-SQL. Python was created by Guido van Rossum, with the first release in 1991. SQL Server 2016 started to support R. In addition, SQL Server 2016 brought all of the infrastructure needed to support additional languages. Therefore, it was easy for SQL Server 2017 to add support for Python. In the future, SQL Server might support even more programming languages. I will explain the SQL Server infrastructure later in this chapter. Anyway, it is now up to you to select your language of preference for data science projects.

One of the most important ideas behind Python was code readability. In Python, white spaces are used to delimit code blocks instead of special characters, and indents are very important. As an interpreted language, Python has automatic memory management. For the sake of simplicity, it has a dynamic type system. The Python syntax allows you to use the program paradigm you prefer—**procedural**, **object-oriented**, or **functional** programming. as with R, there are Python interpreters for all major operating systems. The non-profit Python Software Foundation manages CPython, the reference implementation of Python. Although probably not as rich as in R, there is a huge set of additional libraries available for Python. Nevertheless, the standard libraries included in the Python installation that comes with SQL Server are typically powerful enough for most of the data science projects. Unlike R, I will not install any additional libraries for Python for the demo code I wrote for this book.

This chapter will cover the following topics:

- Selecting the Python environment
- Starting with basic Python
- Understanding Python data structures
- Machine-Learning Services integration with SQL Server

Selecting the Python environment

Once you've installed ML Services (in-database), in `Chapter 1`, *Writing Queries with T-SQL*, and Visual Studio 2017 for data science and analytical applications, in `Chapter 2`, *Introducing R*, you need to create the appropriate VS 2017 Python environment. VS 2017 installs the Anaconda Python, an open source Python distribution, that does not include Microsoft libraries. You need to select the Python distribution that comes with SQL Server, ML Services (In-database). There is no need for such a step for R , because VS 2017 also installs Microsoft R Client. As you should remember from `Chapter 2`, *Introducing R*, Microsoft R Client is the open R engine distributed by Microsoft, and this version includes the Microsoft scalable libraries.

After you install VS 2017, your default Python environment is Anaconda. You need to add an additional **Python environment**. This new environment must point to the scalable version of the interpreter. If you used the defaults when installing SQL Server, the path is `C:\Program Files\Microsoft SQL Server\MSSQL14.MSSQLSERVER\PYTHON_SERVICES\python.exe`. The following screenshot shows how to set up this additional Python environment:

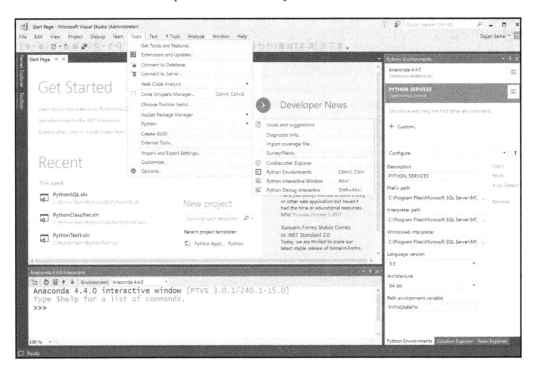

Setting up an additional Python environment

You might also consider marking this environment as default for new Python projects. You are ready to go. Start a new project and select the Python application template from the `Python` folder. You can take some time to explore the Python Machine-Learning templates. With R, there are no specific templates available in VS 2017. For Python, besides other general-purpose programming templates, you can find the templates for the classifier, clustering, and regression projects. For the purpose of executing demo code from this book, use the Python application template, where you get an empty Python script with a default name that is the same as the project name, and the `.py` default extension. As with R scripts, you can use this Python script to write and interactively execute Python code.

Writing your first python code

Let me start with commenting your code. Use the hash mark for a comment the same way you use it in R. In Visual Studio, you use the *Ctrl* and *Enter* keys to execute a line of code where the cursor is, or to execute a marked block of code. I will start with the `print()` command to print some strings. Both single and double apostrophes are string delimiters. Here is the first Python code:

```
# This is a comment
print("Hello World!")
# This line is ignored - it is a comment again
print('Another string.')
print('O"Brien') # In-line comment
print("O'Brien")
```

When you execute the code, the **Python Interactive** window opens (if it is not open yet), located by default below the **Script** window, at the bottom of the screen. This is again very similar to R, to the R console window.

You can combine multiple strings and expressions in a single `print()` statement. For expressions, Python supports all regular mathematical and comparison operators, and executes them in accordance with rules from mathematics and logic, like other programming languages. The following code shows some expressions:

```
3 + 2
print("The result of 5 + 30 / 6 is:", 5 + 30 / 6)
10 * 3 - 6
11 % 4
print("Is 8 less or equal to 5?", 8 <= 5)
print("Is 8 greater than 5?", 8 > 5)
```

Here are the results. If you executed the code by yourself, you probably noticed Python repeats each line of code in the console window before showing the result of this line. I deleted the rows with code to get more readable results:

```
5
The result of 5 + 30 / 6 is: 10.0
24
3
Is 8 less or equal to 5? False
Is 8 greater than 5? True
```

Python is case-sensitive, just like R. This is true also for your variable names. You can see how to assign values to variables and then use those variables in the following code. Note that in Python, you use a single assignment operator, the equals (=) operator:

```
# Integer
a = 3
b = 4
a ** b
# Float
c = 6.0
d = float(7)
print(c, d)
```

As you saw, both double and single quotes serve as string delimiters. You can use single quotes inside a double-quoted string, and the opposite, as I have already shown, for writing O'Brien. When you format a string in the `print()` statement, you can use the `%?` operator to include variables. The question mark in this syntax is a wild character replacing a single letter that denotes the data type of the variable. Use s for strings and d for numbers. You to do variable substitutions in a string with the `str.format()` method of the string datatype. Here are some examples:

```
# Variables in print()
e = "repeat"
f = 5
print("Let's %s string formatting %d times." % (e, f))
# String.format()
four_par = "String {} {} {} {}"
print(four_par.format(1, 2, 3, 4))
print(four_par.format('a', 'b', 'c', 'd'))
```

The result of the previous code is this:

```
Let's repeat string formatting 5 times.
String 1 2 3 4
String a b c d
```

A string can span multiple lines. You need to enclose such long strings in a pair of three double quotes. If you want to use a special character in your string, such as the tab and line feed characters, you need to escape them with a single backslash character and then use a specific letter. You use the letter t for a tab and n for a line feed. You can see some examples in the following code:

```
print("""Three double quotes
are needed to delimit strings in multiple lines.
You can have as many lines as you wish.""")
a = "I am 5'11\" tall"
b = 'I am 5\'11" tall'
print("\t" + a + "\n\t" + b)
```

Here are the results:

```
Three double quotes
are needed to delimit strings in multiple lines.
You can have as many lines as you wish.
   I am 5'11" tall
   I am 5'11" tall
```

In Python, help is always at your fingertips, just use the help() command.

You can create your modules of code. A Python module is a text file with Python code, using the .py extension by default. You can import a module into your current script with the import command. After the module is imported, the functions and the variables defined in that module are available in your script. Modules are a good way to reuse code.

Using functions, branches, and loops

You can encapsulate your code inside a function. The def name(): command defines a function name and is the first code in your function definition. Functions include zero or more parameters and can return values. The following is an example of two functions. The first one has no parameters. The second one has two parameters and returns a value. There is no special ending mark of a function body—as you know, the correct indentation is important. Indentation tells the Python interpreter where the body of one function ends and the next command starts:

```
def nopar():
    print("No parameters")
def add(a, b):
    return a + b
```

When you call a function, you can pass arguments for the parameters as literals, or through variables. You can even do some operations on the arguments when you pass them to the function. The following code shows these possibilities:

```
# Call without arguments
nopar()
# Call with variables and math
a = 10
b = 20
add(a / 5, b / 4)
```

Here are the results:

```
No parameters
7.0
```

The `if..elif..else:` statement is used in Python for branching the flow of your code. Here is an example of not-so-elementary branching:

```
a = 10
b = 20
c = 30
if a > b:
    print("a > b")
elif a > c:
    print("a > c")
elif (b < c):
    print("b < c")
    if a < c:
        print("a < c")
    if b in range(10, 30):
        print("b is between a and c")
else:
    print("a is less than b and less than c")
```

The results of the branching code are shown here. Could you determine the output without executing the code or looking at the result? Take a look at the following:

```
b < c
a < c
b is between a and c
```

I will introduce the simplest data structure in Python, the `list`, before the next section, where you will learn about data frames and other structures. I need it to show you how to create loops.

A Python list is a set of comma-separated values (or items) between square brackets. You can use the `for each` loop to iterate over a list. There are many methods supported by a list. For example, you can use the `list.append()` method to append an element to a list. You can also use the basic `for` loop to iterate some code a specific number of times. The following code shows how to create a list. Then it shows the `for element in list` loop (for each) and the `for` loop . Finally, there is the `while` loop:

```python
animals = ["bee", "whale", "cow"]
nums = []
for animal in animals:
    print("Animal: ", animal)
for i in range(2, 5):
    nums.append(i)
print(nums)
i = 1
while i <= 3:
    print(i)
    i = i + 1
```

Here are the results:

```
Animal: bee
Animal: whale
Animal: cow
[2, 3, 4]
1
2
3
```

Another basic data structure is the `dictionary`. This is a set of the **key–value** pairs. Here is an example of a dictionary:

```python
CtyCou = {
    "Paris": "France",
    "Tokyo": "Japan",
    "Lagos": "Nigeria"}
for city, country in CtyCou.items():
    print("{0} is in {1}.".format(city, country))
```

Here are the results:

```
Lagos is in Nigeria.
Paris is in France.
Tokyo is in Japan.
```

I mentioned that in Python you can also use the object-oriented paradigm. However, going deeper into object-oriented programming with Python is outside the scope of this book, which is, as you know, focused on data science with SQL Server and related tools.

Organizing the data

I want to start this section by showing you some of Python's analytical and graphic capabilities. I am explaining the code just briefly here; you will learn more about Python data structures very quickly. Let's start coding! First, I need to import the necessary libraries:

```
import numpy as np
import pandas as pd
import pyodbc
import matplotlib.pyplot as plt
```

For the data I will analyze, I am using the data from the AdventureWorksDW2017 demo database, selecting from the dbo.vTargetMail view, like I did in Chapter 2, *Introducing R*, when I introduced the R language. I am also using ODBC to connect to SQL Server, with the same data source name and SQL Server login as I did then:

```
con = pyodbc.connect('DSN=AWDW;UID=RUser;PWD=Pa$$w0rd')
query = """SELECT CustomerKey,
            Age, YearlyIncome,
            CommuteDistance, BikeBuyer
        FROM dbo.vTargetMail;"""
TM = pd.read_sql(query, con)
```

You can get quick info about the data with the following code, which shows the first five rows and the number of rows and columns:

```
TM.head(5)
TM.shape
```

Now I need to define CommuteDistance as a discrete, or categorical, variable with an internal order:

```
TM['CommuteDistance'] = TM['CommuteDistance'].astype('category')
TM['CommuteDistance'].cat.reorder_categories(
  ["0-1 Miles",
  "1-2 Miles","2-5 Miles",
  "5-10 Miles", "10+ Miles"], inplace=True)
```

The next step is a cross-tabulation of the `CommuteDistance` variable by the `BikeBuyer` variable:

```
cdbb = pd.crosstab(TM.CommuteDistance, TM.BikeBuyer)
cdbb
```

The first useful result is a `pivot` table of the two cross-tabulated variables:

```
BikeBuyer            0    1
CommuteDistance
0-1 Miles         2772 3538
1-2 Miles         1703 1529
2-5 Miles         1395 1839
5-10 Miles        1896 1318
10+ Miles         1586  908
```

A graph is much more readable than a `pivot` table. So let me create a graph:

```
cdbb.plot(kind = 'bar',
          fontsize = 14, legend = True,
          use_index = True, rot = 1)
plt.show()
```

You can see the graph I produced in the following screenshot:

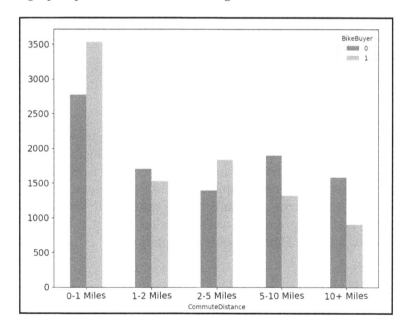

Graph from the cross-tabulation

Let's go into the details of the code I used. I imported the NumPy library, which is short for Numerical Python; the library name is numpy. The library brings arrays that use a very efficient storage. They work much faster than basic lists and dictionaries. A numpy array must have elements of a single data type, just like R arrays. I imported the numpy package with the np alias. Now I will check the version of the library, and then create two one-dimensional arrays from two lists, one with an implicit element-datatype integer, and one with an explicit float datatype:

```
np.__version__
np.array([1, 2, 3, 4])
np.array([1, 2, 3, 4], dtype = "float32")
```

Here are the results:

```
'1.12.1'
array([1, 2, 3, 4])
array([ 1., 2., 3., 4.], dtype=float32)
```

Arrays can be multidimensional. I will create three new arrays, with three rows and five columns each. I will fill the first one with zeros, the second one with ones, and the third one with the number pi. I am using the numpy functions for these assignments:

```
np.zeros((3, 5), dtype = int)
np.ones((3, 5), dtype = int)
np.full((3, 5), 3.14)
```

Let me show you only the last array here:

```
array([[ 3.14, 3.14, 3.14, 3.14, 3.14],
       [ 3.14, 3.14, 3.14, 3.14, 3.14],
       [ 3.14, 3.14, 3.14, 3.14, 3.14]])
```

The numpy library includes many more functions that help you with array population. The arange() function creates a sequence. The upper bound is not included in the array; the range is an interval closed on the left side and open on the right side. Use the random.random() function to generate uniformly-distributed numbers. The random.normal() function generates numbers with the normal (Gaussian) distribution with a specific mean and standard deviation. The random.randint() function generates uniformly-distributed integers. Here are some examples:

```
np.arange(0, 20, 2)
np.random.random((1, 10))
np.random.normal(0, 1, (1, 10))
np.random.randint(0, 10, (3, 3))
```

The arrays generated are shown here. Please note that, except for the first array, you should get different numbers than I did, because they are, as mentioned, random numbers:

```
array([ 0,  2,  4,  6,  8, 10, 12, 14, 16, 18])
array([[ 0.9259839 , 0.14149764, 0.40489916, 0.29531834, 0.91569126,
         0.93224104, 0.91185772, 0.11457454, 0.51763041, 0.95998268]])
array([[ 0.64050407, 0.13393019, 0.03176633, -0.42997222, -0.29441129,
         0.06254568, 0.73507341, -0.68556645, -1.07465048, 0.61561997]])
array([[3, 6, 3],
       [0, 6, 2],
       [1, 7, 8]])
```

The `numpy` library also includes **vectorized** versions of basic functions and operators that work on scalar values. The vectorized ones operate on vectors and matrices as a whole. This is much faster than looping over arrays and operating with basic operators element by element. Here is an example of a numpy vectorized function:

```
x = np.arange(0, 9).reshape((3, 3))
x
np.sin(x)
```

Here is the result:

```
array([[0, 1, 2],
       [3, 4, 5],
       [6, 7, 8]])
array([[ 0.        ,  0.84147098,  0.90929743],
       [ 0.14112001, -0.7568025 , -0.95892427],
       [-0.2794155 ,  0.6569866 ,  0.98935825]])
```

You can also use the numpy aggregate functions. For a data science project, it is crucial to understand the data. You need to do an overview of your data. Descriptive statistics are very handy for this task. Numpy includes both regular aggregate functions and statistical functions. Here is an example of an array:

```
x = np.arange(1,6)
x
```

The content of the array is as follows:

```
array([1, 2, 3, 4, 5])
```

I am using the numpy functions to calculate the sum and the product of the elements, the minimum and the maximum, and the mean and the standard deviation:

```
np.sum(x), np.prod(x)
np.min(x), np.max(x)
np.mean(x), np.std(x)
```

Here are the results:

```
(15, 120)
(1, 5)
(3.0, 1.4142135623730951)
```

You can also calculate running aggregates, such as a running total:

```
np.add.accumulate(x)
```

The running total result is here:

```
array([ 1,   3,   6,  10,  15], dtype=int32)
```

The possibilities of the numpy package are not exhausted yet. However, I am switching to the next important library, the Pandas library.

The pandas library is built on the top of the numpy library—it uses numpy arrays and functions. To import pandas, you need to import numpy first. The pandas library brings the data structures that are used for data science datasets. The first important one is the pandas **Series** object. This is a one-dimensional array, like the numpy array, but more powerful. Besides the implicit positional index, you can define an explicitly-named index. Then you can refer to that name to retrieve the data. A pandas series object resembles a tuple in the relational model. The following example code creates a simple pandas Series, without an explicit index, so you can refer to elements through the positional index only:

```
ser1 = pd.Series([1, 2, 3, 4])
ser1[1:3]
```

Here are the results. Note that the results could be a bit confusing. The upper bound is not included, and the index is zero-based. Therefore, positions 1:3 refer to the second and the third element; the first element with position 0 is not included, and the forth element with position 3 is not in the result either:

```
1    2
2    3
```

It is less confusing to work with an explicit index, as the following code shows:

```
ser1 = pd.Series([1, 2, 3, 4],
                 index = ['a', 'b', 'c', 'd'])
ser1['b':'c']
```

As you can see from the last example, you can refer to elements using the names of the index, which serve as column names in a SQL Server row. Note that the upper bound in the range, the index position named c, is with an explicitly-named index included in the result:

```
b    2
c    3
```

The pandas **DataFrame** object is like a multiple series, each one with the same number of elements, arranged like columns in a table. The Pandas data frame is very similar to the R data frame. You use the pandas data frame for analyses. When you read the data from relational sources, such as SQL Server, you store it in a data frame. You can export a data frame to the tabular destinations, like relational databases. When I read SQL Server data at the beginning of this section, I read the tabular data in a Python data frame. The main difference, compared to an SQL Server table, is that a data frame is a matrix, meaning that you still can refer to the data by the position, and that the order of the data is meaningful and preserved.

The Pandas data frame has many methods. You have already seen the graphic capabilities of it in the beginning of this section, when I used the plot() method to create a bar chart. In addition, you can use the data frame's descriptive statistics functions for your data overview. The next example demonstrates the usage of the describe() function on the whole data frame to calculate basic descriptive statistics on every single column. Then I calculate the mean, standard deviation, skewness, and kurtosis, that is, the first four population moments, with specific functions for this calculation:

```
TM.describe()
TM['YearlyIncome'].mean(), TM['YearlyIncome'].std()
TM['YearlyIncome'].skew(), TM['YearlyIncome'].kurt()
```

Let me finish this section with another diagram. The following code shows the distribution of the YearlyIncome variable binned in 25 bins in histograms and with a kernel density plot:

```
(TM['YearlyIncome']).hist(bins = 25, normed = True,
                          color = 'lightblue')
(TM['YearlyIncome']).plot(kind='kde',
                          style='r--', xlim = [0, 200000])
plt.show()
```

Take a look the following diagram:

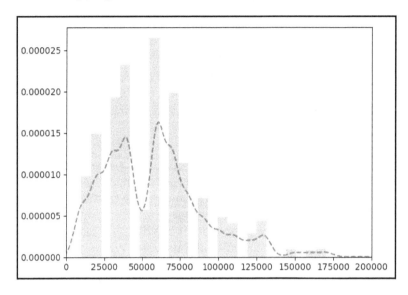

Figure 3.3: Histogram and kernel density plot

Before finishing this chapter, let me explain how the R and Python language support is integrated in SQL Server.

Integrating SQL Server and ML

Of course, you already know that you can execute R and Python code from the T-SQL code. With SQL Server 2016 and 2017, you get a highly scalable ML engine. You install this engine with SQL Server installation by selecting the ML Services (In-database), as I explained in Chapter 1, *Writing Queries with T-SQL*. With Microsoft libraries, you get a lot of parallelized functions that utilize this scalable engine. You can use these functions for huge datasets. You can store a machine-learning model created with R or Python in a SQL Server table in a binary column. You use the stored models for predictions on new data. If you save an R or Python graph to a binary column, you can use it in **SQL Server Reporting Services** (**SSRS**) reports. Besides SQL Server, other Microsoft products and services support Python and R Power BI Desktop, Power BI Service, and Azure Machine Learning, or Azure ML, support both languages.

You can acquire two versions of the Microsoft ML:

- **ML Services (In-database)**: This is the engine that integrates with SQL Server, the one I explained how to install in `Chapter 1`, *Writing Queries with T-SQL*. It adds another service that runs outside the SQL Server Database Engine and provides a communication between the Database Engine and ML Engine.
- **Microsoft ML Server**: This is a standalone ML server. You can acquire this one if you don't need SQL Server. It includes the same open and scalable packages and it runs on multiple platforms.

The most important Microsoft packages shipped with SQL Server ML Services are as follows:

- **RevoScaleR (for R) and Revoscalepy (for Python)**: A library of parallelized scalable functions you can use for data processing, data overview, and data science models. The procedures in this package don't need to load all of the data in memory immediately. They know how to work with chunks of data at a time. This way, they can consume really huge datasets.
- **MicrosoftML (for R) and microsoftml (for Python)**: This is a newer package that brings many additional scalable machine-learning algorithms.

The communication process between the SQL Server Engine and ML Engine is schematically shown in the following diagram:

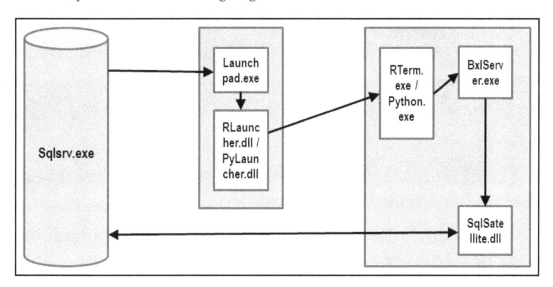

SQL Server and ML Services (in-database)

Here is a brief description of the components and their roles in the communication:

- You start by running the R or Python script in SQL Server with the `sys.sp_execute_external_script` system-stored procedure.
- SQL Server sends the request to the `Launchpad` service. This service was introduced in SQL Server 2016. It supports the execution of external scripts.
- The Launchpad service starts the launcher appropriate for the language of your script, either `RLauncher.dll` or `PyLauncher.dll`. The infrastructure is prepared to enable additional programming languages when needed.
- RLauncher or PyLauncher starts `RTerm.exe`, the R terminal application for executing R scripts, or `Python.exe`, the Python terminal application.
- The terminal application in any of the two languages sends the script to **BxlServer**, or **Binary Exchange Language Server**. It manages the communication between the database and machine-learning engines.
- BxlServer uses SQL Satellite, an API for a fast data transfer between SQL Server and the external runtime.

Before finishing this chapter, I want to show you how you can execute Python and R code inside SQL Server. Now you need to switch to **SQL Server Management Studio (SSMS)**. First, you need to configure your SQL Server to allow external scripts:

```
-- Configure SQL Server to allow external scripts
USE master;
EXEC sys.sp_configure 'show advanced options', 1;
RECONFIGURE WITH OVERRIDE;
EXECsys.sp_configure'external scripts enabled', 1;
RECONFIGURE WITH OVERRIDE;
GO
-- Restart SQL Server
-- Check the configuration
EXEC sys.sp_configure;
GO
```

You can immediately check whether you can run Python code with the `sys.sp_execute_external_script` procedure. The following code returns a 1 x 1 table, with a value of 1 in the single cell:

```
-- Check whether Python code can run
EXECUTE sys.sp_execute_external_script
@language =N'Python',
@script=N'
OutputDataSet = InputDataSet
```

```
print("Input data is: \n", InputDataSet)
',
@input_data_1 = N'SELECT 1 as col';
GO
```

Finally, let me also execute some R code inside SQL Server. With the following code, I am checking the installed R packages:

```
-- Check the installed R packages
EXECUTE sys.sp_execute_external_script
 @language=N'R'
,@script =
 N'str(OutputDataSet)
   packagematrix <- installed.packages()
   NameOnly <- packagematrix[,1]
   OutputDataSet <- as.data.frame(NameOnly)'
,@input_data_1 = N'SELECT 1 AS col'
WITH RESULT SETS (( PackageName nvarchar(250) ));
GO
```

If you execute the previous code, please check that you get in the results the R scalable libraries mentioned in this section.

Summary

After learning the basics of T-SQL and R, you also got an overview of the Python language. When doing the data science tasks, Python resembles R quite a lot. You use the same data frame object to store your data to analyze as in R. You also saw how the integration between SQL Server and ML services works. Now the real work can begin. In the next two chapters, you will see how to get an understanding of your data, and how to prepare it for more advanced analyses.

4
Data Overview

After introducing all of the three languages in the previous three chapters, it is time to do some serious work. Before doing some advanced analysis, you need to understand your data. In this stage, you typically do some preliminary statistical analysis and quite a few data visualizations.

In this chapter, you will learn the following topics:

- A life cycle of a data science project
- Ways to measure data values
- Analyzing continuous variables with descriptive statistics and visualizations
- Analyzing discrete variables with frequency tables and graphs
- Getting a basic idea about the associations between pairs of variables

Getting familiar with a data science project life cycle

A long-term data science project is somehow never finished. It has its own complete life cycle. This virtuous cycle includes the following steps:

1. Identify the business problem
2. Use data mining and machine learning techniques to Transform the data into actionable information
3. Act on the information
4. Measure the result

Data science is not a product. Data science gives you a platform for continuous learning on how to improve your business. In order to learn how to exploit data mining maximally, you need to measure the results of your actions based on the information extracted with data mining. Measurement provides the feedback for continuously improving results. You can see the life cycle in the following diagram:

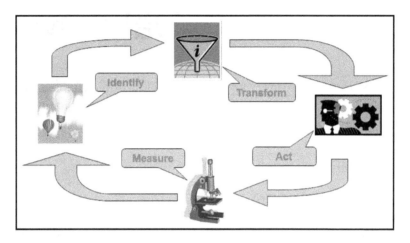

Figure 4.1: Data science project life cycle

Let me give you an example. For credit card issuers and online banking, fraud detection is quite a common task. You want to identify fraudulent transactions as quickly as possible to minimize the damage. You realize that you get some frauds in your system. You identified a problem, so this is the **Identify** part. Then, you use your existing data and implement a data science algorithm on it to get a model. This is the **Transform** part. Then, you use the model to perform online predictions and divert possible fraudulent transactions for an inspection immediately when they appear in your system. This is the **Act** part. Now, you need to close the cycle. You realize that fraudsters learn, and the patterns of frauds can change over time. Therefore, the model you deployed in production might become obsolete. You need to measure the quality of the predictions over time: perform the **Measure** part of the life cycle. When the quality drops, it is time to refine your model. This means you just identified a problem.

Of course, not every project is so complex as the fraud detection is. For a simple one-time marketing campaign, you do not close the loop with the measuring part; once you use the model in production, the project can be closed.

The second step in this life cycle, the step where you transform your data to an actionable knowledge, is the part when you do the most complex work. This is the part that this book focuses on. This part is further divided into steps that can be execute in loops. The **Cross Industry Standard Process for Data Mining** (**CRISP**) model is an informally standardized process for the **Transform** part. It splits the process in six phases. The sequence of the phases is not strict. Moving back and forth between different phases is always required. The outcome of each phase determines the next phase (or particular task of a phase) that has to be performed. The arrows indicate the most important and frequent dependencies between phases. The following diagram depicts the CRISP model:

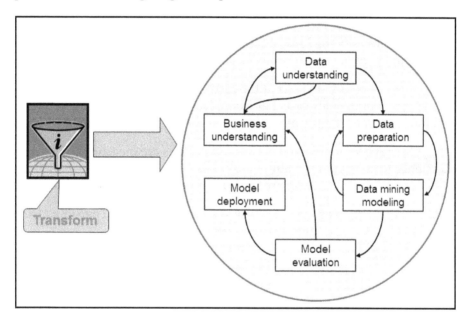

Figure 4.2: The CRISP model

The six CRISP phases should finish with some deliverables. The phases with typical deliverables include the following:

- **Business understanding**: Data-mining problem definition
- **Data understanding**: Data quality reports, descriptive statistics, graphical presentations of data, and so on
- **Data preparation**: Cleansed training and evaluation datasets, including derived variables
- **Modeling**: Different models using different algorithms with different parameters
- **Evaluation**: Decision whether to use a model and which model to use

- **Deployment**: End-user reports, OLAP cube structure, OLTP soft constraints, and so on

You can learn more about this model at `https://en.wikipedia.org/wiki/Cross-industry_standard_process_for_data_mining`.

Ways to measure data values

I already introduced statistical terminology, which is also used in data science: you analyze **cases** using their **variables**. In a RDBMS database, a case is represented as a row in a table and a variable as a column in the same table. In Python and R, you analyze data frames, which are similar to tables, just with positional access.

The first thing you need to decide is what the case is you want to analyze. Sometimes, it is not so easy to exactly define your case. For example, if you're performing a credit risk analysis, you might define a family as a case rather than a single customer.

The next thing you have to understand is how data values are measured in your data set. A typical data science team should include a subject matter expert that can explain the meaning of the variable values. There are several different types of variables:

- **Continuous** variables have an infinitive range of values. There are also couple of different types of continuous variables:
    - **True numeric** have no limits on either the lower bound or the upper bound. They support all arithmetical operations.
    - In business, you often get continuous variables with some limits, at least on one side of the scale. For example, age can't get below zero. Limited continuous variables are **intervals**. They can have only one or two boundaries; they have an order; they allow some arithmetic. For example, think of temperatures. Subtraction makes sense, while summation, most of the time, does not make sense.
    - A continuous variable that increases monotonously, with or without bound, is a **monotonic** variable. Even if such a variable is used just as a key, it might still be interesting to use in your analysis. For example, the ever-growing identification number can tell you something about the time when the case came into the system: lower IDs are usually older than higher IDs. Note that this depends on the source system. Therefore, it is really necessary to contact a subject matter expert before making any conclusions.

- **Discrete** variables have a limited pool of possible values:
  - The values of a discrete variable can be only labels, without natural order. Those are **categorical** or **nominal**. For example, you can denote your mood with couple of distinct values: happy, sad, angry, and so on.
  - If the values of a discrete variable have a natural order, then this is an **ordinal** variable, or a **rank**. Although the order is clear, you cannot use any arithmetic on these values. Typical example of ordinals include all kind of product evaluations, education, and **binned** (grouped, **discretized**) true numeric values.
  - Some categorical variables are very specific. If they can take only one possible value, then they are **constants**. Constants are not interesting for an analysis, because you can always predict the variable value without the analysis. If they can take two possible distinct values, then we call them **dichotomous** variables. If these two values are 0 and 1, then they are also called **binary** variables; if the values are logical values true and false, then they are sometimes called **Boolean** variables. Many times, we want to predict a Boolean variable, for example a decision of a case—yes or no.

Introducing descriptive statistics for continuous variables

A continuous variable can take any value from an interval, or from all real numbers; there is no limit for the number of distinct values here. Of course, you could try to discretize a continuous variable and then treat it as a discrete one. I will discuss different discretization options in the next chapter. In this section, I am going to introduce some statistical measures that describe the distribution of a continuous variable, measures that are called **descriptive statistics**.

You want to understand the distribution of a continuous variable. You can create graphs for all continuous variables. However, comparing tens or even hundreds of graphs visually does not tell you much. You can also describe the distribution numerically, with descriptive statistics. Comparing numbers is much faster and easier than comparing graphs. The you use are the **moments** of a .

The well-known are the **center**, **spread**, **skewness**, and **tailedness** of distribution (I will define these expressions later in this section). You will learn about the following:

- Various measures for centers of a distribution
- Spread of a distribution
- Higher population moments

Calculating centers of a distribution

We are all used to use the term *average* in common speech. For example, in sports, you can hear that the players of a specific team are in average old. The average value somehow describe the cases you are talking about. For example, a higher income average for some group compared to other groups of people might mean that these are richer people. However, as you will learn very soon, the average by itself is not enough to give you a correct estimation of a group. Just one very, very rich person in the group mentioned could shift the average income far to the right on the scale, to the higher values, although all of the other people from that group might be quite poor.

Therefore, we need to measure more than just the average. For measuring the center of the cases you are analyzing, the following are two of the most popular measures:

- The **median** is the value you get in the middle of your sample distribution when you sort cases by the variable for which you are calculating the median. The median splits the cases into two halves: above it and below it. With an odd number of rows, the median is the value in the middle row. If you have an even number of rows in your dataset, then the median is usually calculated as the average value of the two middle rows (the financial median); you can also use the smaller of the two values in the middle (the lower statistical median), or the larger of them (the upper statistical median). For an even number of rows, I will calculate the financial median, and just call it the median. For example, in the set 1, 1, 3, 4, 4, the median is 3, and in the set 1, 2, 3, 4, 5, 6, the median is 3.5.
- The **arithmetic mean** is the famous average. This is the sum of values divided by the number of cases. The arithmetic mean of the series 1, 1, 3, 4, 4 is 2.6. From now on, I will just use the term "mean" for the arithmetic mean.

For good data understanding, you need to calculate more than one center of a distribution. You can get a basic idea of the distribution already by comparing the median and the mean. If the distribution is symmetrical, then the median and the mean are close together, or even coincide. If not, the distribution is skewed in some way.

A distribution is skewed if it has a long tail to the right or to the left. For example, the income distribution might have a long tail on the right side, and might be skewed to the right, with only few very rich people. However, there are many more people with lower income. In such a case, the median would be lower than the mean, because there are more cases on the left than on the right size of the distribution, while the few very high values would raise the value of the mean substantially. If the mean is lower than the median, then you could conclude that your distribution is skewed to the left.

The definition of the mean is, as you already know, the sum of all values divided by the number of cases. Let me introduce the formal formula:

$$\mu = 1/n * \sum_{i=1}^{n} v_i$$

In R and Python, it is even simpler to get the basic descriptive statistics. In R, I used the `summary()` function for a quick overview of the `Age` variable:

```
summary(Age)
```

In the result that follows, you can see that this function returned the minimal and the maximal value, the value on the first and on the third quartile, and the median and the mean. I will explain the other values besides the mean and the median in a minute:

```
   Min. 1st Qu.  Median    Mean 3rd Qu.    Max.
  17.00   24.00   31.00   33.66   41.00   87.00
```

Note that the data in the `AdventureWorksDW2017` is somehow stale, and you might get a different result. I used the following code to make the customers in my database 15 years younger:

```
USE AdventureWorksDW2017;

UPDATE dbo.DimCustomer
  SET BirthDate = DATEADD(year, 15, BirthDate);
```

In Python, there is a similar `describe()` function in the pandas package. Here is the code:

```
TM.Age.describe()
```

This function returns the count of the cases, mean, the standard deviation, the minimal and the maximal value, the value on the first and on the third quartile, and the median as the value at the 50% of the population:

```
count    18484.000000
mean        33.662357
std         11.517815
min         17.000000
25%         24.000000
50%         31.000000
75%         41.000000
max         87.000000
```

You can use more specific functions to calculate just a single value. This is the code that calculates the mean and the median in Python:

```
TM.Age.mean()
TM.Age.median()
```

The R counterpart for the Python code is shown here:

```
mean(Age)
median(Age)
```

In T-SQL, The PERCENTILE_CONT() function calculates a percentile based on a continuous distribution of the column value in SQL Server. The percentile is the input parameter. If you use the value of 0.5 for the percentile, this means that you are searching for the value in the middle, or the median. This function calculates the financial median. The function returns all of the rows with the same value. To get a single value, I use the keyword DISTINCT, like you see in the following code:

```
SELECT DISTINCT
 PERCENTILE_CONT(0.5) WITHIN GROUP (ORDER BY Age) OVER () AS Median
FROM dbo.vTargetMail;
```

The result is 31.

I am not focusing too much on explaining the details of the T-SQL queries, which will become quite more complex later in this chapter. I am focusing on statistical measures here, and showing the code in three different languages. If you want to learn the details about the programming logic of queries like I wrote here, please refer to the book *T-SQL Querying* by Itzik Ben-Gan, Dejan Sarka, Adam Machanic, and Kevin Farlee, Microsoft Press, 2015 (`https://www.pearson.com/us/higher-education/program/Ben-Gan-T-SQL-Querying/PGM254820.html`). I wrote Chapter 8, *T-SQL for BI practitioners of* the book, where I explain the details how to write queries that calculate different statistical measures in T-SQL.

You can use the `AVG()` built-in T-SQL aggregate function to calculate the mean, as the following query shows:

```
SELECT AVG(1.0*Age) AS Mean
FROM dbo.vtargetMail;
```

My result is `33.662356`.

I will stop with the calculations of the centers here. Let me just mention that in the accompanying code for this book, you can find code for even more calculations, including the mode, the geometric, and the harmonic mean.

Measuring the spread

After you have the centers of the distribution, the next interesting question is how spread the values are. Do you have a very homogeneous sample, where the vast majority of the values is close to the mean, or do you have a lot of data far away on both sides of the center?

The **range** is the simplest measure of the spread; it is just the difference between the maximal value and the minimal value of a variable. Writing this definition as a formula is shown here:

$$R = v_{max} - v_{min}$$

In R, you can simply use the `min()` and the `max()` function from the base installation to calculate the range.

```
min(Age)
max(Age)
range(Age)
```

The result is 70. Here is the equivalent code in Python:

```
TM.Age.min()
TM.Age.max()
TM.Age.max() - TM.Age.min()
```

Of course, you use the MAX() and MIN() T-SQL aggregate functions to calculate the range of a variable:

```
SELECT MAX(Age) - MIN(Age) AS Range
FROM dbo.vTargetMail;
```

Instead of splitting the distribution in two halves to get the median, you can split the distribution in many more parts, which are called **quantiles**. If you divide it into four parts, you get **quartiles**; these are the three values that split the data set into quarters (at 25%, 50%, and 75% of all rows). The second quartile is on the half of the data set—this is the median. The first quartile is also called the lower quartile and the third one the upper quartile. The **inter-quartile range (IQR)** is defined as the upper quartile value minus the lower quartile value:

$$IQR = Q_3 - Q_1$$

In R, you can use the built-in function IQR() to calculate the inter-quartile range, and the quantile() function to get the value at the specific quantile.

```
quantile(Age, 1 / 4)
quantile(Age, 3 / 4)
IQR(Age)
```

In Python, you calculate IQR manually with the help of the quantile() method:

```
TM.Age.quantile(0.25)
TM.Age.quantile(0.75)
TM.Age.quantile(0.75) - TM.Age.quantile(0.25)
```

Similar for the median, you can also use the PERCENTILE_CONT() function in T-SQL to calculate the IQR:

```
SELECT DISTINCT
 PERCENTILE_CONT(0.75) WITHIN GROUP (ORDER BY 1.0*Age) OVER () -
 PERCENTILE_CONT(0.25) WITHIN GROUP (ORDER BY 1.0*Age) OVER () AS IQR
FROM dbo.vTargetMail;
```

The IQR is like the median resistant to big oscillations in the values, because the lowest and the highest values are not used in the calculation. You use only two key observations. When the range is much higher than the inter-quartile range, this means that some values are far away from the mean.

Imagine you have a single observation (n=1) only. The mean of this dataset is equal to the value of this single case, and the spread is zero. Calculating the spread makes sense if you have more than one observation. Therefore, only the (n–1) pieces of information are helpful for the spread. This number (n-1) is called the **degrees of freedom**. Degrees of freedom tell you how many pieces of information can vary. The last piece is fixed. Think of a variable that can take four distinct states only. The cumulative percentage for all four values is 100. When you know the frequencies of any three states, you can calculate the fourth frequency; therefore, this one is determined by the other three.

Variance measures the sum of the squared deviations from the mean, considering the degrees of freedom as well. Squared deviations are used because some deviations are negative and some positive, and the basic sum would be zero. The formula for the variance (**Var**) is as follows:

$$Var = 1/(n-1) * \sum_{i=1}^{n}(v_i - \mu)^2$$

This is the formula for the **variance of a sample**, when you deal with samples and not with whole population, or census. This is very typical for statistics. You can use this variance as the estimator for the **variance of the population**. However, if you have census data, then the formula for the variance of the population does not consider the degrees of freedom:

$$VarP = 1/n * \sum_{i=1}^{n}(v_i - \mu)^2$$

For large samples, the difference between Var and VarP is neglectable.

The **standard deviation (σ)** is defined as the square root of the variance. This is the most popular measure for the spread. With the square root, it compensates for the squares in the variance. The formula is as follows:

$$\sigma = \sqrt{Var}$$

Since you have two variants of the variance, you have also two variants of the standard deviation, for the sample and for the population.

I introduced the absolute measures of the spread, the interpretation of which is quite evident for a single variable—the bigger the variance or the standard deviation, the more spread. But, how do you compare the spreads of two or more different variables? A relative measure would be handy here. Now, I am introducing the **coefficient of the variation** (**CV**), which is a simple division of the standard deviation with the mean value:

$$CV = \sigma/\mu$$

In T-SQL, you get functions for calculating everything: the VARP() function is for calculating the variance of the population, the VAR() function is for calculating the variance of the sample, the STDEVP() for calculating the standard deviation for the population, and the STDEV() function for calculating the standard deviation for a sample, which you can use as an estimator for the standard deviation for the population. The following query is therefore quite simple and straightforward. It calculates standard deviations and the coefficients of the variation for the Age and YearlyIncome variables:

```
SELECT STDEV(1.0*Age) AS StDevAge,
  STDEV(1.0*YearlyIncome) AS StDevIncome,
  STDEV(1.0*Age) / AVG(1.0*Age) AS CVAge,
  STDEV(1.0*YearlyIncome) / AVG(1.0*YearlyIncome) AS CVIncome
FROM dbo.vTargetMail;
```

Here are the results:

```
StDevAge            StDevIncome         CVAge               CVIncome
----------------    ----------------    ----------------    ----------------
11.5178146121881    32285.8417029682    0.342157114974011   0.563395923529214
```

You can see that although the standard deviation for YearlyIncome is much higher than for Age, the mean of YearlyIncome is also much higher than the mean of Age, and so the coefficient of the variation is not that much different.

Let me calculate the variance, the standard deviation, and the coefficient of the variation for the Age variable in R:

```
var(Age)
sd(Age)
sd(Age) / mean(Age)
```

As always, the same calculation in Python comes as well:

```
TM.Age.var()
TM.Age.std()
TM.Age.std() / TM.Age.mean()
```

As I said, a population can be skewed, or can be thin in the middle and have long tails. How do you measure the skewness and the kurtosis? It's time to switch to the next topic, to the higher population moments.

Higher population moments

Before dealing with two higher population moments, namely with the **skewness** and the **kurtosis**, let's briefly discus the **normal** and **standard normal distributions**.

The normal distribution is the most important distribution in statistics. The shape of this distribution is the famous **bell curve**. A normal distribution is symmetric, with more observations close to the middle than in the tails. In honor of Karl Friedrich Gauss, the distribution is also called the **Gaussian distribution**, and the curve the **Gaussian curve**.

The formula for the normal distribution includes the mean and the standard deviation:

$$f(x, \mu, \sigma) = 1/\sqrt{2\pi}\sigma * e^{-(x-\mu)^2/2\sigma^2}$$

If you do not know the distribution of a variable in advance, you start with an assumption that it follows the normal distribution.

The **standard normal distribution**, also called the **Z distribution**, is a normal distribution standardized around the mean of 0 and with a standard deviation of 1. The following formula normalizes the x values of the normal distribution:

$$z = (x - \mu)/\sigma$$

You can see an example of a normal distribution in the following screenshot:

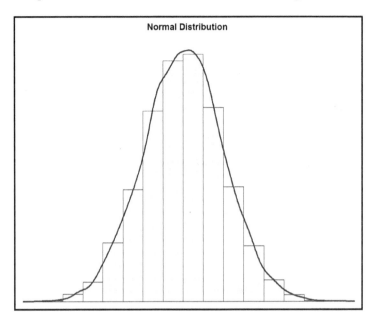

Figure 4.3: The bell curve

The area under the curve between two standard deviations away from the mean on each side covers around 95% of population. This means that only 2.5% of cases are under each tail, or only 5% under both tails. Therefore, if an observation lies quite far away from the mean, for example four standard deviations away, supposing the distribution is normal, this observation is somehow suspicious. This could be an outlier: a rare and far-out-of-bounds value. It might be just an error in your data, or a real outlier.

Skewness is a measure that describes asymmetry in the probability distribution. It shows you the level of asymmetry of a distribution around the mean. If the skewness is positive, the distribution has a longer tail on the right side of the mean. Negative skewness indicates the opposite—an asymmetric tail extending toward the values lower than the mean.

If you have s skewed distribution, then the cases that are quite far away from the mean could still be valid. With positive skewness, you can accept higher values as valid, the values under the right tail of the distribution curve, and with negative skewness you can accept values quite far away from the mean on the left side.

It's time to introduce the formula for the skewness:

$$Skew = n/((n-1)*(n-2)) * \sum_{i=1}^{n}((v_i - \mu)/\sigma)^3$$

You can see an example of a positively skewed distribution in the following screenshot:

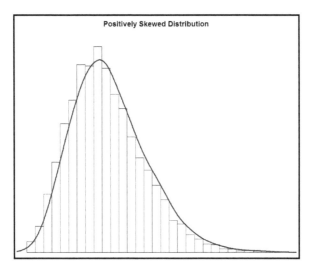

Figure 4.4: Positively skewed distribution

What if a distribution has long tails on both sides? Then you can use the **kurtosis**. Kurtosis tells you something about the relative tailednes of a distribution compared with the normal distribution. A positive kurtosis means there are some some extreme values on one or both sides from the mean, that there is a long tail on one or both sides. The distribution could be quite narrow around the mean, having a peak. However, the tail values bring much more to the calculation; therefore, it is not necessary that a distribution with positive kurtosis has a high peak as well. A negative kurtosis indicates short tails, with probably a relatively flat distribution near the mean value. For a tailed distribution, consider that values far from the mean in any direction might be correct. The formula for the kurtosis is as follows:

$$Kurt = (n*(n+1))/((n-1)*(n-2)*(n-3)) * \sum_{i=1}^{n}((v_i - \mu)/\sigma)^4 - (3*(n-1)^2)/((n-2)*(n-3))$$

The following screenshot shows a tailed distribution, also, in this example, with a peak:

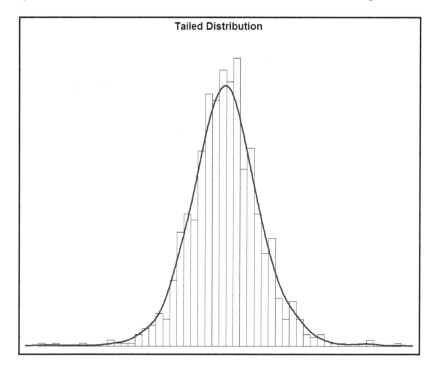

Figure 4.5: Tailed distribution

There are no functions for calculating skewness and kurtosis in basic R. Naturally, you can get them in some additional packages. However, you can also write a custom function. I will use this opportunity to show you how to write a function in R. My function calculates the skewness and the kurtosis. Here is the code, including the call of the function with the Age variable as the argument:

```
skewkurt <- function(p) {
 avg <- mean(p)
 cnt <- length(p)
 stdev <- sd(p)
 skew <- sum((p - avg) ^ 3 / stdev ^ 3) / cnt
 kurt <- sum((p - avg) ^ 4 / stdev ^ 4) / cnt - 3
 return(c(skewness = skew, kurtosis = kurt))
}
skewkurt(Age)
```

Here is the result:

```
    skewness     kurtosis
 0.70826579  -0.02989311
```

Since the skewness is positive, it means that the Age variable has a longer tail on the right side than on the left side of the mean. However, the skewness is quite small, so the right tail is not very long. The result for the kurtosis is very close to zero. You can say that the distribution of the Age variable does not differ much from the normal distribution.

In Python, the pandas library includes the function for calculating skewness and kurtosis, so the code is shorter than in R:

```
TM.Age.skew()
TM.Age.kurt()
```

There are no statistical functions to calculate the skewness and the kurtosis in T-SQL. However, it is possible to calculate them with quite efficient queries. Here is an example of how to calculate the skewness efficiently:

```
WITH SkewCTE AS
(
SELECT SUM(1.0*Age) AS rx,
 SUM(POWER(1.0*Age,2)) AS rx2,
 SUM(POWER(1.0*Age,3)) AS rx3,
 COUNT(1.0*Age) AS rn,
 STDEV(1.0*Age) AS stdv,
 AVG(1.0*Age) AS av
FROM dbo.vTargetMail
)
SELECT
 (rx3 - 3*rx2*av + 3*rx*av*av - rn*av*av*av)
 / (stdv*stdv*stdv) * rn / (rn-1) / (rn-2) AS Skewness
FROM SkewCTE;
```

Similarly, you can calculate the kurtosis with just as efficient a query:

```
WITH KurtCTE AS
(
SELECT SUM(1.0*Age) AS rx,
 SUM(POWER(1.0*Age,2)) AS rx2,
 SUM(POWER(1.0*Age,3)) AS rx3,
 SUM(POWER(1.0*Age,4)) AS rx4,
 COUNT(1.0*Age) AS rn,
 STDEV(1.0*Age) AS stdv,
 AVG(1.*Age) AS av
FROM dbo.vTargetMail
```

```
)
SELECT
 (rx4 - 4*rx3*av + 6*rx2*av*av - 4*rx*av*av*av + rn*av*av*av*av)
 / (stdv*stdv*stdv*stdv) * rn * (rn+1) / (rn-1) / (rn-2) / (rn-3)
 - 3.0 * (rn-1) * (rn-1) / (rn-2) / (rn-3) AS Kurtosis
FROM KurtCTE;
```

Before finishing this chapter, I want to give you a taste of intermediate-level analysis. In addition, for a break after this long section with code and numbers only, I will show you some graphs.

Using frequency tables to understand discrete variables

For an overview of discrete variables, you use `frequency` tables and charts. A frequency table can show the following:

- The values
- The count of the values, or the absolute frequency
- The proportion of the value, or the absolute percentage
- The cumulative frequency
- The cumulative percent
- Plus, you can create a **bar chart** or a **histogram** of the values' absolute percentage

Minimally, you need to calculate the counts of the distinct values of the variable.

Let me start with calculating the frequencies with T-SQL. Window aggregate functions are very handy here. The following query is a very efficient one. If you look at the first part of the query, you'll notice that there is a common table expression (CTE) query that calculates the absolute numbers, or the counts. The cumulative values—the running totals—are calculated with the help of window aggregate functions.

The query calculates the frequencies of the `CommuteDistance` variable from the `dbo.vTargetMail` view from the `AdventureWorksDW2017` database. Note that this variable, although it is a string, has an intrinsic order; it is an ordinal. I need to change the values to define the correct order with the help of the `CASE` T-SQL expression:

```
USE AdventureWorksDW2017;
WITH freqCTE AS
(
SELECT CASE v.CommuteDistance
```

```
        WHEN '0-1 Miles' THEN '1 - 0-1 Miles'
    WHEN '1-2 Miles' THEN '2 - 1-2 Miles'
        WHEN '2-5 Miles' THEN '3 - 2-5 Miles'
        WHEN '5-10 Miles' THEN '4 - 5-10 Miles'
    WHEN '10+ Miles' THEN '5 - 10+ Miles'
      END AS CommuteDistance,
 COUNT(v.CommuteDistance) AS AbsFreq,
 CAST(ROUND(100. * (COUNT(v.CommuteDistance)) /
      (SELECT COUNT(*) FROM vTargetMail), 0) AS INT) AS AbsPerc
FROM dbo.vTargetMail AS v
GROUP BY v.CommuteDistance
)
SELECT CommuteDistance,
 AbsFreq,
 SUM(AbsFreq)
  OVER(ORDER BY CommuteDistance
      ROWS BETWEEN UNBOUNDED PRECEDING
     AND CURRENT ROW) AS CumFreq,
 AbsPerc,
 SUM(AbsPerc)
  OVER(ORDER BY CommuteDistance
      ROWS BETWEEN UNBOUNDED PRECEDING
     AND CURRENT ROW) AS CumPerc,
 CAST(REPLICATE('*',AbsPerc) AS VARCHAR(50)) AS Histogram
FROM freqCTE
ORDER BY CommuteDistance;
```

The following screenshot shows the result:

	CommuteDistance	AbsFreq	CumFreq	AbsPerc	CumPerc	Histogram
1	1 - 0-1 Miles	6310	6310	34	34	**********************************
2	2 - 1-2 Miles	3232	9542	17	51	*****************
3	3 - 2-5 Miles	3234	12776	17	68	*****************
4	4 - 5-10 Miles	3214	15990	17	85	*****************
5	5 - 10+ Miles	2494	18484	13	98	*************

Figure 4.6: Frequencies with the T-SQL result

Now I will use R to calculate the frequencies of the NumberCarsOwned variable from the same view. First, let's read the data:

```
library(RODBC)
con <- odbcConnect("AWDW", uid = "RUser", pwd = "Pa$$w0rd")
TM <-
sqlQuery(con,
 "SELECT CustomerKey,
```

```
    TotalChildren, NumberChildrenAtHome,
    Gender, HouseOwnerFlag,
    NumberCarsOwned, MaritalStatus,
    Age, YearlyIncome, BikeBuyer,
    EnglishEducation AS Education,
    EnglishOccupation AS Occupation
    FROM dbo.vTargetMail;")
close(con)
```

You can use the `table()` function from the core R to get the counts:

```
table(TM$NumberCarsOwned)
```

Here are the results. Note that this variable can be treated as a continuous interval with the lower bound equal to zero or as a discrete ordered variable, or ordinal. I am using it as an ordinal here. I do not need to define the order—the values themselves are correctly defining the order (normally, because they are integers):

```
   0    1    2    3    4
4238 4883 6457 1645 1261
```

In R, you can **attach** a data frame. This means you are adding it to the internal search path. After that, you can refer to the variables with their names only; you do not need to write the variables with the data frame name and the dollar sign prefix. Variable names of the data frames included in the search path must be unique. I am doing this with the following line of code:

```
attach(TM)
```

The `Education` variable is also discrete, but, the variable is a string. R sorts strings in the alphabet order by default. Therefore, I need to inform R about the correct order. I am using the `factor()` function for this task. Then the code uses the `plot()` function to generate a bar chart. Note that I refer in the code to the `Education` variable by using its name only, not the `TM$Education` format, because I attached the TM data frame to the search path:

```
Education = factor(Education, order = TRUE,
  levels = c("Partial High School",
  "High School", "Partial College",
  "Bachelors", "Graduate Degree"))
plot(Education, main = 'Education',
  xlab = 'Education', ylab = 'Number of Cases',
  col = "purple")
```

You can see the plot in the following screenshot:

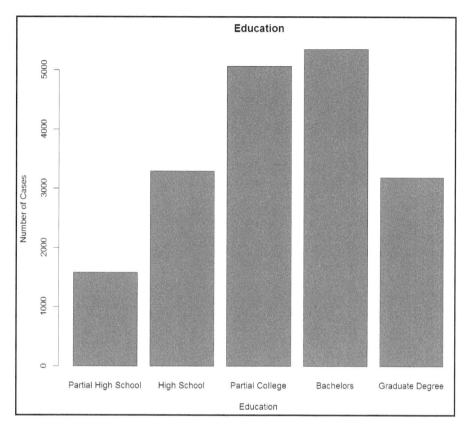

Figure 4.7: Education bar chart

As you already know, there are always many ways how to do something in R. For frequencies and other descriptive statistics, you can use the `descr` package. The following code installs this package, loads it in memory, and calculates the frequencies for the `Education` variable:

```
install.packages("descr")
library(descr)
freq(Education)
```

The `freq()` function provides both textual and graphical results. I am showing the textual results only because the graph is the same as the one in the previous diagram:

```
Education
                    Frequency Percent Cum Percent
Partial High School      1581   8.553       8.553
High School              3294  17.821      26.374
Partial College          5064  27.397      53.771
Bachelors                5356  28.976      82.747
Graduate Degree          3189  17.253     100.000
Total                   18484 100.000
```

Let me switch to Python. The following code first imports the libraries I am going to use in this chapter, and then reads the data from SQL Server:

```python
import numpy as np
import pandas as pd
import pyodbc
import matplotlib as mpl
import matplotlib.pyplot as plt
import seaborn as sns

con = pyodbc.connect('DSN=AWDW;UID=RUser;PWD=Pa$$w0rd')
query = """SELECT CustomerKey,
 TotalChildren, NumberChildrenAtHome,
 Gender, HouseOwnerFlag,
 NumberCarsOwned, MaritalStatus,
 Age, YearlyIncome, BikeBuyer,
 EnglishEducation AS Education,
 EnglishOccupation AS Occupation
 FROM dbo.vTargetMail"""
TM = pd.read_sql(query, con)
```

You already know that you can create graphs with pandas. In the previous code, you can see that I imported some libraries I did not describe yet. Let me introduce them.

You will learn how to do graphs with two Python libraries: matplotlib and seaborn. Both of them are included in the Python version shipped with SQL Server ML Services (In-database). Matplotlib is a cross-platform graphics engine, used as a backbone for many other graphical functions from other libraries. Besides importing this library, you need also to import an interface to it.

Matplotlib is the whole library. `Matplotlib.pyplot` is a module in matplotlib, which is the interface to the underlying plotting library. Unlike with R, where the graph was sent to the screen automatically, you need to call the `show()` function from the pyplot interface to open the graphical window with your graph. One of the visualization libraries built on matplotlib is the seaborn library. This library adds enhanced graphing options, and makes working with pandas data frames easy and coding quite simple.

To get the absolute frequencies, you can use the pandas `value_counts()` function. For example, you could do this for the `Education` variable:

```
TM['Education'].value_counts()
```

If you executed the previous line, you could notice that the order of the `Education` values is not correct. Just as with R, you need to also inform Python about the correct order of the values. Let me define the variable as a categorical one, and reorder the values and calculate the counts properly:

```
TM['Education'] = TM['Education'].astype('category')
TM['Education'].cat.reorder_categories(
 ["Partial High School",
 "High School","Partial College",
 "Bachelors", "Graduate Degree"], inplace=True)
TM['Education'].value_counts().sort_index()
```

Here are the results:

```
Partial High School     1581
High School             3294
Partial College         5064
Bachelors               5356
Graduate Degree         3189
```

Here is another example of the pandas `plot()` function. First, you need to store the counts in an object, and then you plot this object. The code stores the plot in the `ax` object and then adds the labels. Finally, it shows the plot:

```
edu = TM['Education'].value_counts().sort_index()
ax = edu.plot(kind = 'bar',
 color = ('b'),
 fontsize = 14, legend = False,
 use_index = True, rot = 1)
ax.set_xlabel('Education', fontsize = 16)
ax.set_ylabel('Count', fontsize = 16)
plt.show()
```

I am again not showing the plot here, because it is the same as the bar chart created with R in the previous figure. I will show you a different bar chart. This time, I am using the seaborn `countplot()` function:

```
sns.countplot(x="Education", hue="BikeBuyer", data=TM);
plt.show()
```

I used two variables in the function; I am showing the counts of `BikeBuyer` distinct values in the groups of different Education levels. This is already more than just a simple bar chart; you can already notice some small association between the two variables—people with higher education tend to buy more bikes. You can see the graph in the following screenshot:

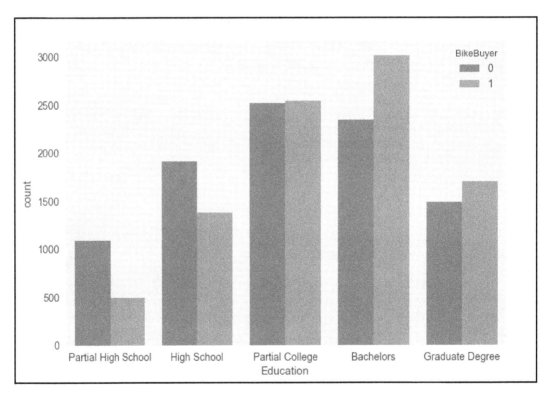

Figure 4.8: Bike buyers at different education levels

I will discuss associations more in-depth later in this chapter. Let me now switch to data overview for continuous variables.

Showing associations graphically

This time, I will show you the code in Python only. I will discuss different measures of associations for discrete and continuous variables, and graphical presentation of these associations, in Chapter 6, Intermediate Statistics and Graphs, of this book. The next two graphs are here just for a tease.

A **scatterplot** is quite common representation of a distribution of two continuous variables. Each point in the plane has coordinates defined by the values of these two variables. From the positions of the points, you can get the impression of the distribution of both variables, and also about possible association between them. Here is the Python code that will create a scatterplot for the Age and YearlyIncome variables:

```
TM1 = TM.head(200)
plt.scatter(TM1['Age'], TM1['YearlyIncome'])
plt.xlabel("Age", fontsize = 16)
plt.ylabel("YearlyIncome", fontsize = 16)
plt.title("YearlyIncome over Age", fontsize = 16)
plt.show()
```

Note that in order to have a less cluttered scatterplot, I limited the plotting to the first 200 cases only. Here is the plot:

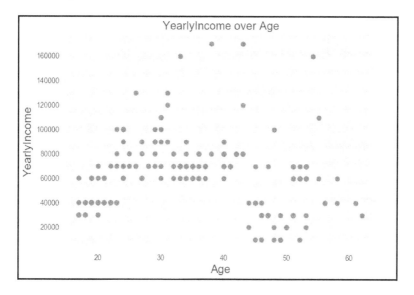

Figure 4.9: Age and YearlyIncome scatterplot

The association between these two variables is quite possible. However, the association might not be a simple linear one. You can notice that the income initially raises with the age; however, later the income decreases with higher age. Actually, the association is polynomial, as I will show you in Chapter 6, Intermediate Statistics and Graphs.

In the seaborn library, you can find the `jointplot()` function. This function shows the joint distribution for two variables in a plane, and the marginal distribution for each one of them on the margins of that plane:

```
with sns.axes_style('white'):
  sns.jointplot('Age', 'YearlyIncome', TM, kind = 'kde')
plt.show()
```

And, the final screenshot for this chapter is shown here:

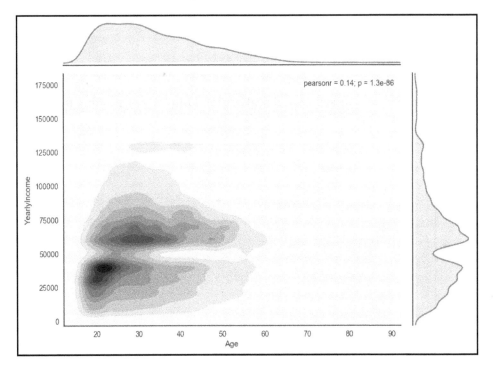

Figure 4.10: Age and YearlyIncome scatterplot

From the preceding screenshot, you can really easily note the distribution of each input variable individually, and whether there is some association between the two of them.

Summary

So, in this chapter, you started with some real work. You were given a brief introduction into statistical measures that describe the distribution of a variable, and how to calculate them in three different languages. This visualization of statistics and data can sometimes already be the final result, and everything you need for a final report. However, in a data science project, this is just an initial step.

In a real-life project, you spend about 70% of the time with data overview and data preparation. This means that there is some more tedious work waiting for you in the next chapter, where I will deal more with the data preparation tasks.

5
Data Preparation

Unfortunately, much of the data you get to work with is not immediately useful for a data science project. A major part of the work on such a project is the data preparation part. There are many different issues you could have with your data. You might have some **missing values** in it. Maybe you need to group some continuous variables in a limited number of **bins**—this means having to **bin** or to **discretize** them. Immediately, you realize that the discretionary is not a particularly straightforward process. Maybe you need to create numerical variables from categorical ones. You create so-called dummy variables, or **dummies**, from values of a categorical variable. Sometimes, you need to **aggregate** data over some **groups** defined with one or more variables, and further operate on aggregated data.

This chapter will introduce you to some of the basic data preparation tasks and tools, including the following:

- Handling missing values
- Creating dummies from categorical variables
- Different ways of discretization
- Measuring the entropy of discretized variables
- Using some advanced packages, expressions, and functions for data preparation

Handling missing values

Let me start by creating and populating a small table with a couple of missing values in some cells, denoted by the reserved word NULL in SQL Server:

```
USE AdventureWorksDW2017;
GO
DROP TABLE IF EXISTS dbo.NULLTest;
GO
CREATE TABLE dbo.NULLTest
(
```

```
    c1 INT NULL,
    c2 INT NULL,
    c3 INT NULL
);
GO
INSERT INTO dbo.NULLTest VALUES
(1, NULL, 3),
(4, 5, 6),
(NULL, 8, 9),
(10, 11, 12),
(13, NULL, NULL);
GO
```

The content of the table is as follows:

```
c1              c2              c3
-----------     -----------     -----------
1               NULL            3
4               5               6
NULL            8               9
10              11              12
13              NULL            NULL
```

In T-SQL, you can use the ISNULL() and COALESCE() functions to work with NULLs. The first one has only two parameters and returns the value of the first parameter, if it is not NULL, and the values of the second parameter otherwise. The second function, just mentioned, accepts multiple parameters and returns the first one that is not NULL. You can see how these two functions work in the following example code:

```
SELECT c1, ISNULL(c1, 0) AS c1NULL,
  c2, c3, COALESCE(c2, c3, 99) AS c2NULL
FROM dbo.NULLTest
```

Here is the result of the previous code:

```
c1              c1NULL          c2              c3              c2NULL
-----------     -----------     -----------     -----------     -----------
1               1               NULL            3               3
4               4               5               6               5
NULL            0               8               9               8
10              10              11              12              11
13              13              NULL            NULL            99
```

T-SQL aggregate functions just skip NULLs, as if they don't exist. The only exception is the COUNT(*) function, which simply counts rows, no matter whether there are some NULLs in various columns. Let me show you an example how this works:

```
SELECT AVG(c2) AS c2AVG, SUM(c2) AS c2SUM, COUNT(*) AS n,
  SUM(1.0*c2)/COUNT(*) AS c2SumByCount
FROM dbo.NULLTest;
```

You can see, in the following result, the difference between the AVG() and SUM()/COUNT(*). I also copied the warning I got together with the results:

```
c2AVG         c2SUM         n             c2SumByCount
-----------   -----------   -----------   ------------
8             24            5             4.800000
Warning: Null value is eliminated by an aggregate or other SET operation.
```

Let me read the same data in R. You should already be familiar with the following code:

```
library(RODBC)
con <- odbcConnect("AWDW", uid = "RUser", pwd = "Pa$$w0rd")
NULLTest <-
sqlQuery(con,
  "SELECT c1, c2, c3
  FROM dbo.NULLTest;")
close(con)
NULLTest
```

As you can see from the result, NULLs are marked in R with NA:

```
   c1  c2  c3
1  1   NA  3
2  4   5   6
3  NA  8   9
4  10  11  12
5  13  NA  NA
```

In R, there are some functions to work with unknown values already in the basic package. You can omit all rows with NAs in any column with the na.omit() function. You can check for the NAs with the is.na() function:

```
na.omit(NULLTest)
is.na(NULLTest)
```

The first line of the code in the previous example returns the second and the fourth rows from the NULLTest data frame. The second line returns the following matrix:

```
   c1     c2     c3
1  FALSE  TRUE   FALSE
2  FALSE  FALSE  FALSE
3  TRUE   FALSE  FALSE
4  FALSE  FALSE  FALSE
5  FALSE  TRUE   TRUE
```

Many functions in R do not work directly with NAs. If you calculate mean on a column with missing values in some rows, the result is unknown. However, many functions also accept the na.rm parameter. When you set this parameter to TRUE, the function skips the rows with missing values, and thus work similarly to the T-SQL aggregate functions. You can see this behavior with the mean() function example:

```
mean(NULLTest$c2)
mean(NULLTest$c2, na.rm=TRUE)
```

The results of the previous two lines of code are as follows:

```
[1] NA
[1] 8
```

There are many other possibilities for how to treat missing values. You might decide to replace the missing values with the average values of the column. You can use any other value as the replacement. You can imagine that there are many other options for handling NAs in R in additional packages. However, this quick guide has to be short; otherwise, it would not be so quick, and therefore I will switch to Python now. The following code imports the modules I will use in this chapter, and reads the demo data for handling NULLs:

```
import numpy as np
import pandas as pd
import pyodbc
import matplotlib as mpl
import matplotlib.pyplot as plt
import seaborn as sns
import scipy as sc
# Demo data
con = pyodbc.connect('DSN=AWDW;UID=RUser;PWD=Pa$$w0rd')
query = """SELECT c1, c2, c3
 FROM dbo.NULLTest;"""
NULLTest = pd.read_sql(query, con)
```

If you check the content of the `NULLTest` Python data frame, you will see that NULLs are marked in Python with the marker NaN. Similar to the `is.na()` function in R, you can check for NaNs in a pandas data frame with the pandas `isnull()` function:

```
pd.isnull(NULLTest)
```

The previous line of code returns a similar True/False matrix, like the `is.na(NULLTest)` function I have just shown in the R examples. You can also omit rows with NaNs in a column, or you can omit columns with NaN in any of the rows:

```
NULLTest.dropna(axis = 'rows')
NULLTest.dropna(axis = 'columns')
```

The first line returns rows 2 and 4, as you can see from the following result, while the second returns an empty data frame, since there is at least one NaN in every single column:

```
    c1    c2    c3
1  4.0   5.0   6.0
3  10.0  11.0  12.0
```

You should never forget to check for unknown values in your data, either in SQL Server tables, or in R and Python data frames.

Creating dummies

Some algorithms, for example, regression analysis algorithms, need numerical input variables. If you want to use a categorical variable in the analysis, you need to convert it somehow to a numerical one. If the variable is ordinal, this is not a problem; you just assign appropriate integers to the naturally ordered values of the variable. From a nominal variable, you can create a set of **indicators**. There is one indicator for each possible value, showing whether the value it represents is taken for a case. If a specific value is taken for a case, you assign 1 to the indicator for this value value, or otherwise 0. Such new variables, the indicators, are also called dummy variables, or dummies. In T-SQL, you can use the `IIF()` function to generate dummies, as the following code shows:

```
SELECT TOP 3 MaritalStatus,
  IIF(MaritalStatus = 'S', 1, 0)
  AS [TM_S],
  IIF(MaritalStatus = 'M', 1, 0)
  AS [TM_M]
FROM dbo.vTargetMail;
```

Here are the results:

```
MaritalStatus TM_S       TM_M
------------- ----------- -----------
M                0           1
S                1           0
S                1           0
```

In Python, you can use the pandas `get_dummies()` function to generate dummies from a variable. This function automatically uses the values of the original variable for the names of the new indicators. You can add a prefix to the names. Before using this function, I need to read the `dbo.vTargetMail` data from the `AdventureWorksDW2017` demo database:

```
con = pyodbc.connect('DSN=AWDW;UID=RUser;PWD=Pa$$w0rd')
query = """SELECT CustomerKey, CommuteDistance,
 TotalChildren, NumberChildrenAtHome,
 Gender, HouseOwnerFlag,
 NumberCarsOwned, MaritalStatus,
 Age, YearlyIncome, BikeBuyer,
 EnglishEducation AS Education,
 EnglishOccupation AS Occupation
 FROM dbo.vTargetMail"""
TM = pd.read_sql(query, con)
```

The following code creates a new data frame that includes only the `MaritalStatus` from the original one, and joins a data frame with dummies created from the `MaritalStatus` variable to it. The second line of the code shows the last three cases of the new data frame:

```
TM1 = TM[['MaritalStatus']].join(pd.get_dummies(TM.MaritalStatus, prefix =
'TM'))
TM1.tail(3)
```

Here are the Python results:

```
      MaritalStatus TM_M TM_S
18481 S                 0    1
18482 M                 1    0
18483 M                 1    0
```

In R, probably the most convenient way for creating dummies is the `dummy()` function from the **dummies** package. But again I need to read the dbo.vTargetMail data first:

```
con <- odbcConnect("AWDW", uid = "RUser", pwd = "Pa$$w0rd")
TM <-
sqlQuery(con,
 "SELECT CustomerKey, CommuteDistance,
 TotalChildren, NumberChildrenAtHome,
```

```
Gender, HouseOwnerFlag, MaritalStatus,
NumberCarsOwned, MaritalStatus,
Age, YearlyIncome, BikeBuyer,
EnglishEducation AS Education,
EnglishOccupation AS Occupation
FROM dbo.vTargetMail;")
close(con)
```

Now I can install the dummies package and call the `dummy()` function to get the same result for the last three rows, as in Python:

```
install.packages("dummies")
library(dummies)
# Create the dummies
TM1 <- cbind(TM, dummy(TM$MaritalStatus, sep = "_"))
tail(TM1[c("MaritalStatus", "TM_S", "TM_M")], 3)
```

You can execute the R code by yourself to check the results.

Discretizing continuous variables

Some algorithms, for example, the Naive Bayes algorithm that will be introduced in Chapter 8, use discrete input variables only. If you want to use a continuous variable in your analysis, you have to discretize it, or bin the values. You might also want to discretize a continuous variable just to be able to show its distribution with a bar chart. There are many possible ways to do the discretization. I will show the following ones:

- Equal width binning
- Equal height binning
- Custom binning

Equal width discretization

Equal width binning is probably the most popular way of doing discretization. This means that after the binning, all bins have equal width, or represent an equal range of the original variable values, no matter how many cases are in each bin. With enough bins, you can preserve the original distribution quite well, and represent it with a bar chart.

I will start with a T-SQL example. I will bin the `Age` variable from the `dbo.vTargetMail` view in five groups with equal width. You might remember from the previous chapter that the minimal age is 17 years, the maximum 87 years, and the range is 70 years. If we split this into five bins, then the width of each bin is 14 years:

```
DECLARE @binwidth AS NUMERIC(5,2),
 @minA AS INT, @maxA AS INT;
SELECT @minA = MIN(AGE),
 @maxa = MAX(Age),
 @binwidth = 1.0 * (MAX(Age) - MIN(Age)) / 5
FROM dbo.vTargetMail;
SELECT CustomerKey, Age,
 CASE
 WHEN Age >= @minA + 0 * @binwidth AND Age < @minA + 1 * @binwidth
 THEN CAST((@minA + 0 * @binwidth) AS VARCHAR(5)) + ' - ' +
 CAST((@minA + 1 * @binwidth - 1) AS VARCHAR(5))
 WHEN Age >= @minA + 1 * @binwidth AND Age < @minA + 2 * @binwidth
 THEN CAST((@minA + 1 * @binwidth) AS VARCHAR(5)) + ' - ' +
 CAST((@minA + 2 * @binwidth - 1) AS VARCHAR(5))
 WHEN Age >= @minA + 2 * @binwidth AND Age < @minA + 3 * @binwidth
 THEN CAST((@minA + 2 * @binwidth) AS VARCHAR(5)) + ' - ' +
 CAST((@minA + 3 * @binwidth - 1) AS VARCHAR(5))
 WHEN Age >= @minA + 3 * @binwidth AND Age < @minA + 4 * @binwidth
 THEN CAST((@minA + 3 * @binwidth) AS VARCHAR(5)) + ' - ' +
 CAST((@minA + 4 * @binwidth - 1) AS VARCHAR(5))
 ELSE CAST((@minA + 4 * @binwidth) AS VARCHAR(5)) + ' + '
 END AS AgeEWB
FROM dbo.vTargetMail
ORDER BY NEWID();
```

I use the `CASE` T-SQL expression to define the bins. Here are couple of rows from the result:

```
CustomerKey Age         AgeEWB
----------- ----------- -------------
22834       50          45.00 - 58.00
17518       23          17.00 - 30.00
22908       27          17.00 - 30.00
17802       33          31.00 - 44.00
21498       41          31.00 - 44.00
```

 I use the `ORDER BY NEWID()` ordering just to shuffle the rows, to get different examples in the first few rows.

I will show you how you can visualize the distribution of the Age variable with a bar chart when you do an equal width binning. Here is a Python example. I am using the pandas cut() function to create the bins, and then to create the bar chart:

```
TM['AgeEWB'] = pd.cut(TM['Age'], 20)
TM['AgeEWB'].value_counts()
pd.crosstab(TM.AgeEWB,
  columns = 'Count') .plot(kind = 'bar',
  legend = False,
  title = 'AgeEWB20')
plt.show()
```

You can see the bar chart created in the following screenshot:

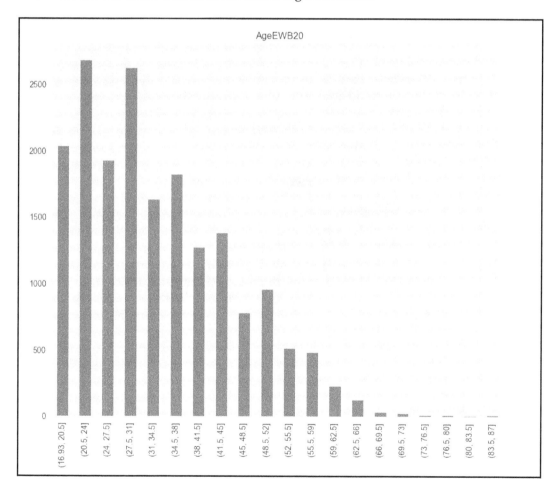

Age distribution in 20 equal width bins

Now, let me perform five bins, as I did in the T-SQL code, and show the counts of the new bins:

```
TM['AgeEWB'] = pd.cut(TM['Age'], 5)
TM['AgeEWB'].value_counts(sort = False)
```

Here are the results:

```
(16.93, 31]  9246
(31, 45]     6089
(45, 59]     2717
(59, 73]      402
(73, 87]       30
```

You can see that the bins, or the intervals, are opened on the left side and closed on the right side. All bins have equal width; however, the number of cases in each bin varies substantially.

In R, there is a function called cut (), implemented in the basic package, that does the equal width binning. The following code also shows the counts, or the absolute frequencies, of the new binned variable:

```
TM["AgeEWB"] = cut(TM$Age, 5)
table(TM$AgeEWB)
```

The results are the same as the results from the Python code.

Equal height discretization

There is a perfectly good reason to perform equal height binning. With this binning, you preserve the maximal possible amount of information that the variable holds, as I will explain later in this chapter. For now, let me just mention again that equal height binning means that after the discretization, each of the new bins has approximately an equal number of cases but a different range.

In T-SQL, you can use the NTILE () function to assign the rows to the tiles. Here is an example:

```
SELECT CustomerKey, Age,
 CAST(NTILE(5) OVER(ORDER BY Age)
 AS CHAR(1)) AS AgeEHB
FROM dbo.vTargetMail
ORDER BY NEWID();
```

The result is shuffled again with the NEWID() function. Here are some rows from the result:

```
CustomerKey Age    AgeEHB
----------- -----  ------
15426          53   5
24403          35   4
19445          29   3
22985          18   1
28064          25   2
```

In R, I create a custom function that does the equal width binning for me. The function calculates how many cases should be in each bin, and then assigns the cases to the bins with the rank() function:

```
EHBinning <- function(data, nofbins) {
 bincases <- rep(length(data) %/% nofbins, nofbins)
 bincases <- bincases + ifelse(1:nofbins <= length(data) %% nofbins, 1, 0)
 bin <- rep(1:nofbins, bincases)
 bin <- bin[rank(data, ties.method = "last")]
 return(factor(bin, levels = 1:nofbins, ordered = TRUE))
}
TM["AgeEHB"] = EHBinning(TM$Age, 5)
table(TM$AgeEHB)
```

Here is the distribution of the cases in the bins:

```
   1    2    3    4    5
3697 3697 3697 3697 3696
```

My function assigns overflow cases to the first bins. The number of cases from my data frame is 18.484; this is not divisible by 5. The remainder of the division is 4. Therefore, I assigned to the first four bins one case more than I did to the last bin. This is the same way as the T-SQL NTILE() function works. Let me show you the distribution of the new AgeEHB variable in a histogram. This time, I am using the scalable rxHistogram() function from the RevoScaleR package shipped with the Microsoft ML services:

```
library("RevoScaleR")
rxHistogram(formula = ~AgeEHB,
 data = TM)
```

From the following screenshot, you can see that the bins have equal height:

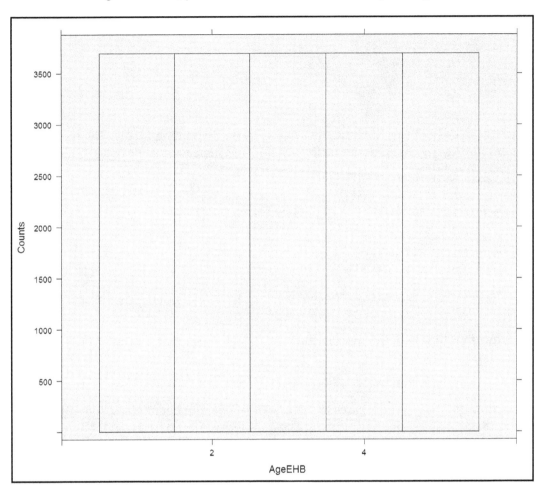

Age distribution in five equal height bins

In Python, you can use the pandas qcut () function for equal height binning. However, this function works slightly differently than the equal height binning I have shown with T-SQL and R. The qcut () function assigns all cases with the same value in a single bin, or a single tile. Therefore, the number of cases in different bins might vary a bit. Here is the Python code:

```
TM['AgeEHB'] = pd.qcut(TM['Age'], 5)
TM['AgeEHB'].value_counts(sort = False)
```

And here are the results:

```
[17, 23] 4059
(23, 29] 3890
(29, 35] 3418
(35, 44] 3702
(44, 87] 3415
```

For the same binning as the NTILE() T-SQL function performs, you can write a custom function in Python, just as I did in R.

Custom discretization

Another very popular way of discretization is the one that somehow tries to follow the real-life context of the values of a variable. Consider income, for example. A 100 units difference (use whatever currency you wish) means a lot when you earn 500 units per month. The same 100 units are not very important if you earn 50,000 units per month. Therefore, it makes sense to make narrower bins at the lower side, and wider ones at the higher side, of the income values. You can implement similar logic when it comes to age. Here is a T-SQL example:

```
SELECT CustomerKey, Age,
 CASE
 WHEN Age >= 17 AND Age < 23
 THEN '17 - 22'
 WHEN Age >= 23 AND Age < 30
 THEN '23 - 29'
 WHEN Age >= 29 AND Age < 40
 THEN '30 - 39'
 WHEN Age >= 40 AND Age < 55
 THEN '40 - 54'
 ELSE '54 +'
 END AS AgeCUB
FROM dbo.vTargetMail
ORDER BY NEWID();
```

Here are a couple of rows from the result:

```
CustomerKey Age     AgeCUB
----------- ------  -------
20204        32     30 - 39
26547        51     40 - 54
19111        25     23 - 29
11190        53     40 - 54
11360        19     17 - 22
14247        55     54 +
```

Both `cut()` functions from R and Python pandas accept a parameter that is a vector of the custom cutting points. Here is the R example:

```
TM["AgeCUB"] = cut(TM$Age, c(16, 22, 29, 39, 54, 88))
table(TM$AgeCUB)
```

Here are the R results:

```
(16,22] (22,29] (29,39] (39,54] (54,88]
 3370    4579    5158    4319    1058
```

The following Python code for the custom binning also creates a bar chart of the new binned variable:

```
custombins = [16, 22, 29, 39, 54, 88]
TM['AgeCUB'] = pd.cut(TM['Age'], custombins)
TM['AgeCUB'].value_counts(sort = False)
pd.crosstab(TM.AgeCUB,
 columns = 'Count') .plot(kind = 'bar',
 legend = False,
 title = 'AgeCUB')
plt.show()
```

The following screenshot shows the distribution of the new discretized variable:

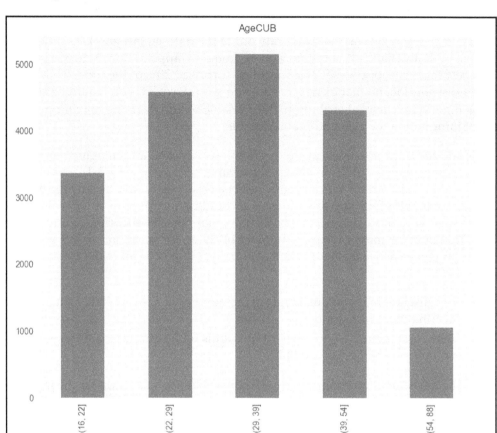

Age distribution in five equal height bins

I promised to explain why the equal height binning preserves the maximum possible information. Therefore, I need to introduce the measure for the information, the entropy.

The entropy of a discrete variable

In the Information Theory, as defined by Claude E Shannon, information is a surprise. Surprise comes from diversity, not from equality. Considering the data, a variable that can occupy a single value only, actually a constant, has no surprise and no information.

Whatever case you take randomly from the dataset, you know the value of this variable in advance, and you are never surprised. To have at least some information in it, a variable must be at least dichotomous, meaning it must have a pool of at least two distinct values. Now, imagine that you take a case randomly out of the dataset, but you know the overall distribution of that variable. If one state is more frequent, appearing in 80% of cases, you would expect that state, of course. You would be surprised 20% of the time. With 50%—50% distribution, no matter which state you would expect, you would be surprised half of the time. With such a distribution, this variable would have the maximum possible amount of information for a dichotomous variable.

Now, let's add the third possible state to our fictitious variable, and imagine that all of the three states have equal distribution, or equal probability, exactly 1/3-1/3-1/3. No matter which state you expect when you randomly select a case, you would be surprised two thirds of the time. With four possible states, you could be surprised even 75% of the time. You can see that with more distinct states, the maximal possible surprise, or information, increases. However, no matter what the number of states, the information in a variable is at the maximum when each state is represented equally. Now you can make two conclusions, as follows:

- With discretizing, you are lowering the number of distinct states, thus also lowering the information in a variable
- When discretizing in equal height bins, bins with equal probability, you preserve as much information as possible

Entropy is the measure of information in a variable. Shannon's formula for the information of a single state is the probability of that state multiplied with the logarithm with base two of this probability:

$$I(x) = -P(x_i) * LOG_2(P(x_i))$$

The negative sign is there because the probability is expressed as a decimal number between 0 and 1, where the logarithm function returns negative values. The entropy of a variable is a sum of information stored in all states of that variable:

$$H(x) = -\sum_{i=1}^{n} P(x_i) * LOG_2(P(x_i))$$

The maximum possible entropy for *n* states is simply as follows:

$$H_{max,n} = LOG_2(n)$$

Here is a T-SQL query that calculates the maximal possible entropy for a couple of different numbers of distinct states:

```
SELECT LOG(2,2) AS TwoStatesMax,
  LOG(3,2) AS ThreeStatesMax,
  LOG(4,2) AS FourStatesMax,
  LOG(5,2) AS FiveStatesMax;
```

The results are as follows:

```
TwoStatesMax  ThreeStatesMax   FourStatesMax       FiveStatesMax
------------  ---------------  ------------------  -----------------------
1             1.58496250072116  2                   2.32192809488736
```

With the maximum possible entropy for a specific number of states known, you can also calculate the **relative entropy** of a variable by simply dividing the actual entropy with the maximum possible one for that variable. Knowing the entropy of discrete variables is also useful for knowing the spread of continuous variables. Variables with more absolute and more relative entropy are more useful for analyses. I guess now you understand why the equal height binning also makes sense. If you have no real-life logic for custom binning, if you don't need to preserve the shape of the distribution, then the equal height binning might be the right choice, because the information loss that comes with the binning is the lowest.

So, let's calculate the entropy for the `CommuteDistance` variable:

```
WITH ProbabilityCTE AS
(
SELECT CommuteDistance,
 COUNT(CommuteDistance) AS StateFreq
FROM dbo.vTargetMail
GROUP BY CommuteDistance
),
StateEntropyCTE AS
(
SELECT CommuteDistance,
 1.0*StateFreq / SUM(StateFreq) OVER () AS StateProbability
FROM ProbabilityCTE
)
SELECT 'CommuteDistance' AS Variable,
  (-1)*SUM(StateProbability * LOG(StateProbability,2)) AS TotalEntropy,
  LOG(COUNT(*),2) AS MaxPossibleEntropy,
  100 * ((-1)*SUM(StateProbability * LOG(StateProbability,2))) /
  (LOG(COUNT(*),2)) AS PctOfMaxPossibleEntropy
FROM StateEntropyCTE;
```

The result of the query is as follows:

```
Variable          TotalEntropy    MaxPossibleEntropy  PctOfMaxPossibleEntropy
---------------   ---------------  ------------------  ----------------------
CommuteDistance  2.2379802017979  2.32192809488736    96.3845610346715
```

You can see that this variable has quite good distribution for analysis purposes.

In Python, you can find the `stats.entropy()` function in the `scipy` package. This is why I imported this package at the beginning of this chapter. However, this function expects as a parameter a series of state probabilities, which I have to calculate in advance. Therefore, I created my own function, `f_entropy()`, as a wrapper around this built-in function:

```
def f_entropy(indata):
  indataprob = indata.value_counts() / len(indata)
  entropy=sc.stats.entropy(indataprob, base = 2)
  return entropy
```

Now I can use my function to calculate the entropy values for two different variables:

```
f_entropy(TM.NumberCarsOwned), np.log2(5), f_entropy(TM.NumberCarsOwned) /
np.log2(5)
f_entropy(TM.BikeBuyer), np.log2(2), f_entropy(TM.BikeBuyer) / np.log2(2)
```

Here are the results:

```
(2.0994297487400737,  2.3219280948873622,  0.9041751781042634)
(0.99989781003755662, 1.0,                 0.99989781003755662)
```

You can see that although the `NumbercarsOwned` variable has higher absolute entropy, the `BikieBuyer` variable has higher relative entropy, nearly as high as the maximum possible entropy for two distinct states.

In R, you can find a function to calculate the entropy in the **DescTools** package. This function expects the counts for the input, as the following code shows:

```
install.packages("DescTools")
library("DescTools")
NCO = table(TM$NumberCarsOwned)
print(c(Entropy(NCO), log2(5), Entropy(NCO) / log2(5)))
BBT = table(TM$BikeBuyer)
print(c(Entropy(BBT), log2(2), Entropy(BBT) / log2(2)))
```

Here are the results:

```
[1] 2.0994297 2.3219281 0.9041752
[1] 0.9998978 1.0000000 0.9998978
```

There are many more data preparation tasks that you might need to perform in a real project. It is impossible to cover all possibilities in a single chapter. However, before finishing this chapter, I want to add a bunch of advanced topics.

Advanced data preparation topics

In the last section of this chapter, I will discuss the following:

- Using the **GROUPING SETS** in T-SQL
- Using the `rx_data_step()` function from the `revoscalepy` Python package
- Introducing the `dplyr` package in R

Efficient grouping and aggregating in T-SQL

In `Chapter 1`, *Writing Queries with T-SQL*, I discussed the core T-SQL SELECT statement clauses, and showed how you can group and aggregate data. But SQL Server has more hidden gems. Maybe you need to create many different groupings and aggregates. In T-SQL, you can help yourself with the `GROUPING SETS` clause.

You could create aggregates over multiple different grouping variables by using multiple `SELECT` statements with a single `GROUP BY` clause for separate grouping, and then you could use the `UNION` clause to return all separate result sets as a single unioned result set. However, you can achieve the same result in a single query with the `GROUPING SETS` clause. You can define multiple sets of variables for grouping, and multiple different grouping variables in every grouping set. SQL Server can analyze this statement and maximally optimize the query. This way, you get very efficient code. Look at the following query:

```
SELECT g.EnglishCountryRegionName AS Country,
 GROUPING(g.EnglishCountryRegionName) AS CountryGrouping,
 c.CommuteDistance,
 GROUPING(c.CommuteDistance) AS CommuteDistanceGrouping,
 STDEV(c.YearlyIncome) / AVG(c.YearlyIncome)
 AS CVIncome
FROM dbo.DimCustomer AS c
 INNER JOIN dbo.DimGeography AS g
 ON c.GeographyKey = g.GeographyKey
GROUP BY GROUPING SETS
 (
  (g.EnglishCountryRegionName, c.CommuteDistance),
```

```
      (g.EnglishCountryRegionName),
      (c.CommuteDistance),
      ()
    )
    ORDER BY NEWID();
```

In a single query, I am calculating the coefficient of variation for the yearly income over countries and commute distance, over countries only, over commute distance only, and over all the dataset. I use ordering by NEWID() again to shuffle the result, to get some interesting rows at the top of the result:

```
Country   CountryGrouping CommuteDistance CommuteDistanceGrouping CVIncome
--------- --------------- --------------- ----------------------- -----
Germany   0               1-2 Miles       0
0.38024260939205
Canada    0               2-5 Miles       0
0.256495601560545
Australia 0               10+ Miles       0
0.21006411302351
NULL      1               2-5 Miles       0
0.485625821896517
France    0               NULL            1
0.762738849203167
France    0               2-5 Miles       0
0.742631239050475
NULL      1               5-10 Miles      0
0.474036351026419
NULL      1               NULL            1
0.563395924217412
```

As you can see in the query, I also used the GROUPING() function. This function tells you whether there is a NULL in a column because this row is an aggregate of NULLs in the raw data of this column, or whether this is a hyper-aggregate over some other variable where the variable used as a parameter for the GROUPING() function makes no sense. Let me explain this from the result. In the first row of the result, you can see that this is an aggregate for Germany, and the commute distance is between one and two miles. The fourth row is an aggregate for commute distance from two to five miles; the NULL in the Country column is there because this is a hyper-aggregate, where country makes no sense. The fifth row shows the opposite situation—this is an aggregate for France, with all possible commute distances. Note the values of the GROUPING() function in these two rows. Also, look at the last row of the result I am showing here. This is an aggregate over the whole dataset, where neither country nor commute distance make any sense.

Leveraging Microsoft scalable libraries in Python

R was supported in SQL Server already with version 2016, and Python with version 2017. Therefore, it is somehow logical that Python is lagging a bit behind R in SQL Server. You can see this fact by the number of functions supported in the scalable Microsoft libraries for both languages. Although there is the `revoscalepy` library, the counterpart for the `RevoScaleR` library, not all functions from the R library are supported in the Python versions. For example, there is no `rxHistogram()` function in the Python version.

In both versions of the aforementioned libraries, you can find a very powerful function for data preparation. The R version is called `rxDataStep()`, and the Python one `rx_data_step()`. However, again, the Python one does not support all of the parameters of the R one. For an example, I am doing a projection, selecting only two columns from the target mail data frame with this function. Note the filtered rows by the regular index locator, the `iloc()` function. Filtering with the `rx_dat_step()` is one example of a task that is still not supported (as of summer 2018) for this scalable function in Python. Here is the code:

```
from revoscalepy import rx_data_step
TM4 = rx_data_step(input_data=TM.iloc[0:3,],
 vars_to_keep = {'CustomerKey', 'Age', 'AgeCUB'})
TM4
```

The result is as follows:

```
   Age  CustomerKey
0 31.0 11000.0
1 27.0 11001.0
2 32.0 11002.0
```

Note that the column order is turned around in the result. It looks as if the function does not guarantee to preserve the order of the columns of the input data frame. Also, note that the data type of the integer input columns changed to decimal in the output. This is not a problem if you use this function in Python code only. You get a data frame, and you have column names. However, if you call this function inside the `sys.sp_execute_external_script` system procedure in SQL Server, you need to know the exact order of the output columns to consume the output in SQL Server. You define the output shape in the `WITH RESULT SETS` clause of this procedure, where the output column order is fixed. I suggest you explicitly cast the output of the `rx_data_step()` functions to the pandas data frame, where you also fix the column order. You can see how to do this in the following code:

```
EXECUTE sys.sp_execute_external_script
@language =N'Python',
```

```
@script = N'
from revoscalepy import rx_data_step
import pandas as pd
OutputDataSet = rx_data_step(input_data=InputDataSet.iloc[0:3,],
 vars_to_keep = {"CustomerKey", "Age"})
OutputDataSet = pd.DataFrame(OutputDataSet, columns=["CustomerKey",
"Age"])',
@input_data_1 = N'SELECT CustomerKey, Age, MaritalStatus FROM
dbo.vTargetMail;'
WITH RESULT SETS (( CustomerKey INT, Age INT ));
GO
```

Here are the results:

```
CustomerKey Age
----------- ---
11000        31
11001        27
11002        32
```

You can see that this time everything is in order.

Using the dplyr package in R

One of the most popular packages for data preparation in R is the `dplyr` package. The package brings a very consistent, simple, readable, and efficient syntax. You work on data with functions that are somewhat mimicking SQL expressions. Let me start this quick introduction with a projection on a dataset. You do this with the `select()` function of the `dplyr` package. But before that, I am reading slightly different data from SQL Server than I did before, because I want to have the country of the customer also in my data frame:

```
con <- odbcConnect("AWDW", uid = "RUser", pwd = "Pa$$w0rd")
TM <- as.data.frame(sqlQuery(con,
 "SELECT c.CustomerKey,
 g.EnglishCountryRegionName AS Country,
 c.EnglishEducation AS Education,
 c.YearlyIncome AS Income,
 c.NumberCarsOwned AS Cars,
 C.MaritalStatus,
 c.NumberChildrenAtHome
 FROM dbo.DimCustomer AS c
 INNER JOIN dbo.DimGeography AS g
 ON c.GeographyKey = g.GeographyKey;"),
 stringsAsFactors = TRUE)
close(con)
```

The following code installs and loads the `dplyr` package, and then makes a couple of projections on the data frame I just read:

```
install.packages("dplyr")
library(dplyr)
# Projection
head(TM)
head(select(TM, Income:MaritalStatus))
head(select(TM, - Income))
head(select(TM, starts_with("C")))
```

Here, I am just showing the result of the last line:

```
  CustomerKey Country    Cars
1 11000          Australia 0
2 11001          Australia 1
3 11002          Australia 1
4 11003          Australia 1
5 11004          Australia 4
6 11005          Australia 1
```

You can filter a data frame with the `filter()` function. Here is an example:

```
# All data frame has 18484 cases
count(TM)
# 2906 cases with more than 2 cars
count(filter(TM, Cars > 2))
```

You can sort the data with the `arrange()` function, such as the following line of code shows:

```
head(arrange(TM, desc(CustomerKey)))
```

The pipe operator (`%>%`) is the one that makes the code really efficient. You pipe the output of one function into the input of the next function. The process of piping together the data manipulation functions is called **chaining**. Look at the following code that pipes the TM data frame to the `select()` function, and how the result of this function is piped to the input of the filtering, and the result of the filtering is piped to the input for the count calculation:

```
TM %>%
select(starts_with("C")) %>%
filter(Cars > 2) %>%
count
```

With the `mutate()` function, you can change the data frame. In the following example, I am filtering the data frame, then adding two variables—a binary to show whether a partner exists for this person, and the total number of people in the household of this case. Then I make a projection, and then reorder the rows. Finally, I am showing the first six rows of the result:

```
TM %>%
filter(Cars > 0) %>%
mutate(PartnerExists = as.integer(ifelse(MaritalStatus == 'S', 0, 1))) %>%
mutate(HouseHoldNumber = 1 + PartnerExists + NumberChildrenAtHome) %>%
select(CustomerKey, Country, HouseHoldNumber, Cars) %>%
arrange(desc(CustomerKey)) %>%
head
```

Another possible action is aggregating the data. You can make aggregations with the `summarise()` function, as the following code shows:

```
TM %>%
filter(Cars > 0) %>%
mutate(PartnerExists = as.integer(ifelse(MaritalStatus == 'S', 0, 1))) %>%
mutate(HouseHoldNumber = 1 + PartnerExists + NumberChildrenAtHome) %>%
select(CustomerKey, Country, HouseHoldNumber, Cars) %>%
summarise(avgCars = mean(Cars),
  avgHouseHoldNumber = mean(HouseHoldNumber))
```

Of course, you can make aggregations in groups as well by using the `group_by()` function. The following code shows all of the possibilities together, and stores the result in a new data frame called `TM1`:

```
TM1 =
TM %>%
filter(Cars > 0) %>%
mutate(PartnerExists = as.integer(ifelse(MaritalStatus == 'S', 0, 1))) %>%
mutate(HouseHoldNumber = 1 + PartnerExists + NumberChildrenAtHome) %>%
select(CustomerKey, Country, HouseHoldNumber, Cars) %>%
group_by(Country) %>%
summarise(avgCars = mean(Cars),
  avgHouseHoldNumber = mean(HouseHoldNumber)) %>%
arrange(desc(Country))
TM1
```

Here is the result:

```
    Country        avgCars   avgHouseHoldNumber
    <fctr>         <dbl>     <dbl>
1 United States  1.894174 2.380048
2 United Kingdom 2.131072 3.586618
3 Germany        1.863793 3.042241
4 France         1.759346 2.474299
5 Canada         1.850362 2.570394
6 Australia      2.142679 2.839213
```

This is a really powerful piece of code. Let me also show you the results of the code graphically. I am showing the average number of people in a household, and the average number of cars per country, in a scatterplot. Instead of using the basic plot() function, I am creating a nicer graph with the help of the scatterplot() function from the car package:

```
install.packages("car")
library(car)
scatterplot(avgCars ~ avgHouseHoldNumber | Country,
 data = TM1,
 xlab = "HouseHoldNumber Avg", ylab = "Cars Avg",
 main = "Enhanced Scatter Plot",
 cex = 3.5, lwd = 15,
 cex.lab = 1.3,
 xlim = c(2.2, 3.6), ylim = c(1.7, 2.2),
 col = c('red', 'blue', 'green', 'black', 'orange', 'magenta'),
 boxplot = 'xy')
```

You can see the graph created with this code in the following screenshot:

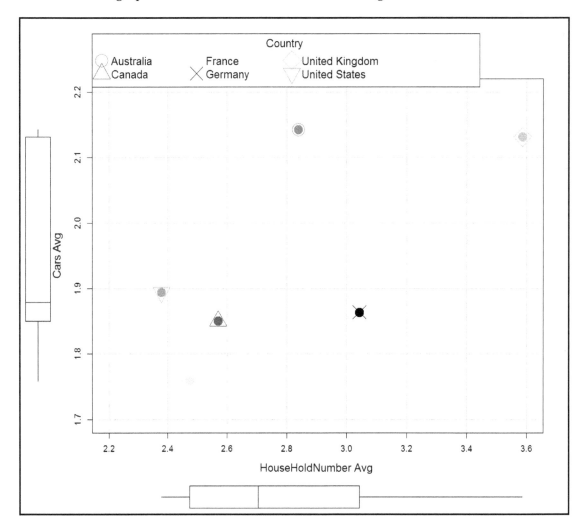

Average number of people in a household and the average number of cars per country

Before finishing this chapter, let me add that you can find some additional examples, in all three languages that I use in this book, in the code associated with the book.

Summary

This was quite a long chapter. However, the chapter still just scratched the surface of possible issues with data preparation. Remember that in a real-life project, you spend the majority of time doing the not-so fun parts: the data preparation and data overview.

In this chapter, you learned the basics of data preparation, including handling missing values, dealing with nominal variables, different ways of discretizing continuous variables, and how to measure the entropy of a discrete variable. At the end, you learned about some efficient ways of performing data manipulation in T-SQL, Python, and R.

The last three chapters of this book are concerned with introducing real analysis of the data. I will start with intermediate-level statistical methods, to explore the associations between variables, and with more advanced graphs.

Intermediate Statistics and Graphs

6

In `Chapter 4`, *Data Overview*, we analyzed a single variable. We finished the chapter by showing possible associations between pairs of variables graphically. In this chapter, I will briefly explain the statistics behind, and then develop the code to measure possible associations between, two variables. I will also include more graphical examples.

A very important concept in statistics is the **null hypothesis**. This is where you start your analysis from; you suppose that there is no association between two variables. An example of a question could be *Is the commute distance to work associated with occupation?* The null hypothesis here is *there is no association between commute distance and occupation*. With statistical analysis, you try either to prove or to reject the null hypothesis. However, you can never be 100% sure of the outcome; therefore, you prove or reject the null hypothesis with some probability.

In this chapter, we will deal with the following topics:

- Exploring associations between continuous variables
- Measuring dependencies between discrete variables
- Discovering associations between continuous and discrete variables
- Expressing dependencies with a linear regression formula

Exploring associations between continuous variables

For a single continuous variable, I introduced a couple of measures for the spread. One of the basic measures for the spread is the variance. If you have two continuous variables, each one has its own variance. However, you can ask yourself whether these two variables vary together. For example, if a value for the first variable of some case is quite high, well above the mean of the first variable, the value of the second variable of the same case could also be above its own mean. This would be a positive association. If the value of the second variable would be lower when the value for the first one is higher, then you would have a negative association. If there is no connection between the positive and negative deviations from the mean for both variables, then you can accept the null hypothesis—there is no association between these two variables. The formula for the **covariance**, which is the first measure for the association I am introducing in this chapter, is as follows:

$$CoVar(X, Y) = 1/n * \sum_{i=1}^{n}(X_i - \mu(X)) * (Y_i - \mu(Y))$$

In the formula, $\mu(X)$ stands for the mean of the variable X, and $\mu(Y)$ for the mean of the variable Y. From the formula, you can see that when the deviation for both variables is positive or negative for many cases, the covariance is positive, showing a positive association; when deviations of one variable are mostly negative for the cases where the deviations of the other variable are positive, the covariance is negative, showing a negative association. If there is no pattern in deviations of both variables, if they are randomly positive or negative for both variables, then the covariance approaches zero, showing there is no association between the two variables in the analysis.

If you remember from Chapter 4, *Data Overview*, the absolute measures for the spread of a variable were not suitable for comparison of spreads between two variables. I introduced a relative measure, the coefficient of variation. You can divide the covariance with the product of the standard deviations of both variables and get the **correlation coefficient**, as the following formula shows:

$$Correl(X, Y) = Covar(X, Y))/((\sigma(X) * \sigma(Y))$$

Correlation can take any value in the interval between -1 and 1. A high negative value means a negative association; a high positive value means a positive association, and when the value is around zero, it means there is no association between the pair of variables analyzed. The question is where is the cut-off point when you can say that the two variables are correlated. An absolute value higher than 0.40 or even 0.50 is quite a safe choice. It is even safer to square this value, which defines the **coefficient of determination**, to diminish the small values and get a safer cutting point. The formula for the coefficient of determination is this:

$$CD(X, Y) = Correl(X, Y)^2$$

When the absolute value for this coefficient is above 0.20, you can safely reject the null hypothesis, and interpret that the two variables are associated.

It's now time to calculate the three measures I introduced. The following T-SQL query checks whether the number of cars owned is correlated with the income. Note that this time I am using the `NumberCarsOwned` variable as a continuous one. With only five distinct integer values between 0 and 4, you can decide by yourself how you will use it—either as a discrete ordinal or as a continuous one:

```
USE AdventureWorksDW2017;
GO
WITH CoVarCTE AS
(
SELECT 1.0*NumberCarsOwned as val1,
 AVG(1.0*NumberCarsOwned) OVER () AS mean1,
 1.0*YearlyIncome AS val2,
 AVG(1.0*YearlyIncome) OVER() AS mean2
FROM dbo.vTargetMail
)
SELECT
 SUM((val1-mean1)*(val2-mean2)) / COUNT(*) AS Covar,
 (SUM((val1-mean1)*(val2-mean2)) / COUNT(*)) /
 (STDEVP(val1)  * STDEVP(val2)) AS Correl,
 SQUARE((SUM((val1-mean1)*(val2-mean2)) / COUNT(*)) /
 (STDEVP(val1)  * STDEVP(val2))) AS CD
FROM CoVarCTE;
GO
```

The result is as follows:

```
Covar           Correl            CD
------------    ------------------ ------------------
17150.222413  0.466647174389393  0.217759585365604
```

As you probably expected, there is a positive association between these two variables.

In R, I will test quite a few variables for the correlation. Let me start again by reading the data:

```
library(RODBC)
con <- odbcConnect("AWDW", uid = "RUser", pwd = "Pa$$w0rd")
TM <-
sqlQuery(con,
 "SELECT CustomerKey, CommuteDistance,
 TotalChildren, NumberChildrenAtHome,
 Gender, HouseOwnerFlag,
 NumberCarsOwned, MaritalStatus,
 Age, BikeBuyer, Region,
 YearlyIncome AS Income,
 EnglishEducation AS Education,
 EnglishOccupation AS Occupation
 FROM dbo.vTargetMail")
close(con)
```

Next, I will check the covariance and the correlation between income and age. I am using the `cov()` and `cor()` functions from the basic R installation:

```
x <- TM[, c("Income", "Age")]
cov(x)
cor(x)
```

Here is the result:

```
        Income      Age
Income 1.042376e+09 53669.9443
Age    5.366994e+04 132.6713
        Income Age
Income 1.0000000 0.1443214
Age    0.1443214 1.0000000
```

You can see that the result comes in a matrix format. If a variable is correlated with itself, then the correlation coefficient is normally 1. You can read the actual correlation coefficient for these two variables in the top-right or bottom-left corner of the lower matrix from the result. The coefficient is less than 0.15. This is quite a small value. You probably expected a higher correlation, that older people earn more than younger people. So, what's going on here? Stay tuned; I will explain the actual association between age and income in the last section of this chapter.

I can calculate the correlation between two vectors of variables, as follows:

```
y <- TM[, c("NumberCarsOwned", "NumberChildrenAtHome")]
cor(y, x)
```

Here is the full matrix of correlation coefficients:

```
                       Income     Age
NumberCarsOwned        0.4666472  0.18380481
NumberChildrenAtHome   0.4521331 -0.01007598
```

You can say that the number of cars owned and the number of children at home are both positively correlated with the income, while the correlations with the age are not that clear. Especially for the number of children at home, you can safely say that it is not associated with the age in this dataset.

You can nicely visualize the correlations with the `corrgram()` function from the `corrgram` package. Install the package only if you did not install it before:

```
z <- TM[, c("NumberCarsOwned", "NumberChildrenAtHome", "Age")]
# install.packages("corrgram")
library(corrgram)
corrgram(z, order = TRUE, lower.panel = panel.shade,
 upper.panel = panel.shade, text.panel = panel.txt,
 cor.method = "pearson", main = "Corrgram")
```

You can see the result in the following diagram:

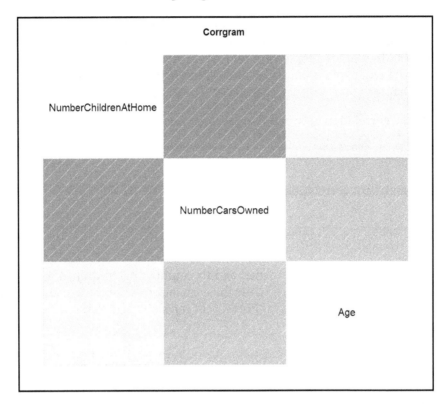

Figure 6.1: Correlations shown graphically

The blue color shows positive associations, and the red color negative ones. The darker the color, the higher the association.

Let me calculate the same coefficients, also in Python. First, I have to import the necessary libraries for this chapter and read the data:

```
# Imports
import numpy as np
import pandas as pd
import pyodbc
import matplotlib as mpl
import matplotlib.pyplot as plt
import seaborn as sns
# Reading the data from SQL Server
con = pyodbc.connect('DSN=AWDW;UID=RUser;PWD=Pa$$w0rd')
query = """SELECT CustomerKey, CommuteDistance,
```

```
     TotalChildren, NumberChildrenAtHome,
     Gender, HouseOwnerFlag,
     NumberCarsOwned, MaritalStatus,
     Age, BikeBuyer, Region,
     YearlyIncome AS Income,
     EnglishEducation AS Education,
     EnglishOccupation AS Occupation
     FROM dbo.vTargetMail"""
TM = pd.read_sql(query, con)
```

Now, I can use the `cov()` function and the `corrcoef()` function from the `numpy` library:

```
np.cov(TM.Age, TM.Income)
np.corrcoef(TM.Age, TM.Income)
```

Here is the result:

```
array([[ 1.32671264e+02, 5.36699443e+04],
 [ 5.36699443e+04, 1.04237557e+09]])
array([[ 1. , 0.14432135],
 [ 0.14432135, 1. ]])
```

Again, you can see the result in a two-dimensional array, or a matrix. The following code shows how to select a single value:

```
np.cov(TM.Age, TM.Income)[0][1]
np.corrcoef(TM.Age, TM.Income)[0][1]
```

The three measures I introduced in this section are not useful for the discrete variables. Therefore, I need to discuss different ones.

Measuring dependencies between discrete variables

You can pivot, or cross-tabulate two discrete variables. You measure counts, or absolute frequencies, of each combination of pairs of values of the two variables. You can compare the **actual** with the **expected** values in the table. So, what are the expected values? You start with the null hypothesis again—there is no association between the two variables you are examining. For the null hypothesis, you would expect that the distribution of one variable is the same in each class of the other variable, and the same as the overall distribution in the dataset. For example, if you have half married and half single people in the dataset, you expect such a distribution for each level of education. The tables where you show the actual and the expected frequencies are called **contingency tables**.

Contingency tables show you only visual dependencies. The numerical measure for the association of two discrete variables is the **chi-squared** value. You calculate this value by calculating the squares of the deviations of the actual from the expected frequencies, and divide this with the expected frequencies. Here is the formula:

$$\chi^2 = 1/n * \sum_{i=1}^{n}(O - E)^2/E$$

You also need to calculate the degrees of freedom with the following formula:

$$DF = (C - 1) * (R - 1)$$

Degrees of freedom for a contingency table is simply the product of the degrees of freedom for columns and for rows. Now you have two numbers, the chi-squared and the degrees of freedom. How to interpret them? You can use the tables with the precalculated values for the **chi-squared critical points** for specific degrees of freedom. The following screenshot shows such a table:

DF	Chi-squared Value										
1	0.004	0.02	0.06	0.15	0.46	1.07	1.64	2.71	3.84	6.64	10.83
2	0.10	0.21	0.45	0.71	1.39	2.41	3.22	4.60	5.99	9.21	13.82
3	0.35	0.58	1.01	1.42	2.37	3.66	4.64	6.25	7.82	11.34	16.27
4	0.71	1.06	1.65	2.20	3.36	4.88	5.99	7.78	9.49	13.28	18.47
5	1.14	1.61	2.34	3.00	4.35	6.06	7.29	9.24	11.07	15.09	20.52
6	1.63	2.20	3.07	3.83	5.35	7.23	8.56	10.64	12.59	16.81	22.46
7	2.17	2.83	3.82	4.67	6.35	8.38	9.80	12.02	14.07	18.48	24.32
8	2.73	3.49	4.59	5.53	7.34	9.52	11.03	13.56	15.51	20.09	26.12
9	3.32	4.17	5.38	6.39	8.34	10.66	12.24	14.68	16.92	21.67	27.88
10	3.94	4.86	6.18	7.27	9.34	11.78	13.44	15.99	18.31	23.21	29.59
Probability	**0.95**	**0.90**	**0.80**	**0.70**	**0.50**	**0.30**	**0.20**	**0.10**	**0.05**	**0.01**	**0.001**
	Not significant								*Significant*		

Figure 6.2: chi-squared critical points

The probability row tells you what the probability is for a chi-squared value greater or equal to the critical point for specific degrees of freedom for two random variables. For example, if you have six degrees of freedom and a chi-squared greater than or equal to 12.59, there is less than a five percent of probability that the differences between observed and expected frequencies are random. You can reject the null hypothesis with 95 percent or more probability. Typically, you say that the the association is significant when there is a less than five percent of probability for accepting the null hypothesis. Nowadays, you don't need to read the tables anymore; you can find many chi-squared calculators for free on the web, such as this one: https://www.mathsisfun.com/data/chi-square-calculator.html.

 I am not trying to advertise any specific site; I just used the first useful link I found.

The following T-SQL code tests the association between occupation and gender:

```
WITH
ObservedCombination_CTE AS
(
SELECT EnglishOccupation AS OnRows,
 Gender AS OnCols,
 COUNT(*) AS ObservedCombination
FROM dbo.vTargetMail
GROUP BY EnglishOccupation, Gender
),
ExpectedCombination_CTE AS
(
SELECT OnRows, OnCols, ObservedCombination
 ,SUM(ObservedCombination) OVER (PARTITION BY OnRows) AS ObservedOnRows
 ,SUM(ObservedCombination) OVER (PARTITION BY OnCols) AS ObservedOnCols
 ,SUM(ObservedCombination) OVER () AS ObservedTotal
 ,CAST(ROUND(SUM(1.0 * ObservedCombination) OVER (PARTITION BY OnRows)
 * SUM(1.0 * ObservedCombination) OVER (PARTITION BY OnCols)
 / SUM(1.0 * ObservedCombination) OVER (), 0) AS INT) AS
ExpectedCombination
FROM ObservedCombination_CTE
)
SELECT SUM(SQUARE(ObservedCombination - ExpectedCombination)
 / ExpectedCombination) AS ChiSquared,
 (COUNT(DISTINCT OnRows) - 1) * (COUNT(DISTINCT OnCols) - 1) AS
DegreesOfFreedom
FROM ExpectedCombination_CTE
```

Here are the results:

```
ChiSquared        DegreesOfFreedom
---------------   ----------------
8.73118071755612  4
```

You can read from the table in the previous figure that the association is not significant, although this insignificance is not really convincing.

Before showing the examples in R, I am asking myself whether the occupation is really a categorical variable, or whether maybe I can define some intrinsic order. The order does not have any influence on the chi-squared calculations, but might be helpful in the future. I could define the order based on some other variable, for example, income. Let me test the means of these two variables in the classes of occupation:

```
SELECT EnglishOccupation,
 AVG(YearlyIncome) AS Income
 FROM dbo.vTargetMail
 GROUP BY EnglishOccupation
 ORDER BY Income;
```

Here is the result of the query:

```
EnglishOccupation Income
----------------- ----------
Manual            16451.3422
Clerical          30710.3825
Skilled Manual    51715.0972
Professional      74184.7826
Management        92325.2032
```

You can see that that the difference in income between different occupations is quite high. Therefore, it may make sense to define the occupation as an ordinal variable. Let me do that in R, together with defining the proper order for the commute distance:

```
# Order CommuteDistance
TM$CommuteDistance = factor(TM$CommuteDistance, order = TRUE,
 levels = c("0-1 Miles",
 "1-2 Miles", "2-5 Miles",
 "5-10 Miles", "10+ Miles"))
# Let's order the Occupation according to the Income
TM$Occupation = factor(TM$Occupation, order = TRUE,
 levels = c("Manual",
 "Clerical","Skilled Manual",
 "Professional", "Management"))
```

Now, let me cross-tabulate these two variables:

```
xtabs(~TM$Occupation + TM$CommuteDistance)
```

Here is the result:

```
                  TM$CommuteDistance
TM$Occupation   0-1 Miles 1-2 Miles 2-5 Miles 5-10 Miles 10+ Miles
Manual            1271       529       541        43          0
Clerical          1706       656       239       300         27
Skilled Manual    1373      1053       695      1226        230
Professional      1217       425      1373      1142       1363
Management         743       569       386       503        874
```

You might notice that the higher the occupation level, the more it leads to a longer commute distance. Therefore, it looks as if these two variables are associated. Let's calculate the chi-squared for these two, and also for occupation and gender:

```
# Storing tables in objects
tEduGen <- xtabs(~TM$Education + TM$Gender)
tOccCdi <- xtabs(~TM$Occupation + TM$CommuteDistance)
# Test of independece
chisq.test(tEduGen)
chisq.test(tOccCdi)
```

The results are as follows:

```
data: tEduGen
X-squared = 5.8402, df = 4, p-value = 0.2114
data: tOccCdi
X-squared = 4587.7, df = 16, p-value < 2.2e-16
```

As you probably expected from the cross-tabulation, commute distance is associated with occupation. Let me also show this graphically. This time, I will use the `ggplot()` function from the `ggplot2` package, probably the most popular graphical package in R:

```
# install.packages("ggplot2")
library(ggplot2)
ggplot(TM, aes(x = CommuteDistance, fill = Occupation)) +
  geom_bar(stat = "count") +
  scale_fill_manual(values = c("yellow", "blue", "red", "green", "black")) +
  theme(text = element_text(size = 15));
```

Please refer to the help for the `ggplot()` functions for the details of the function's parameters.

The following diagram shows the output:

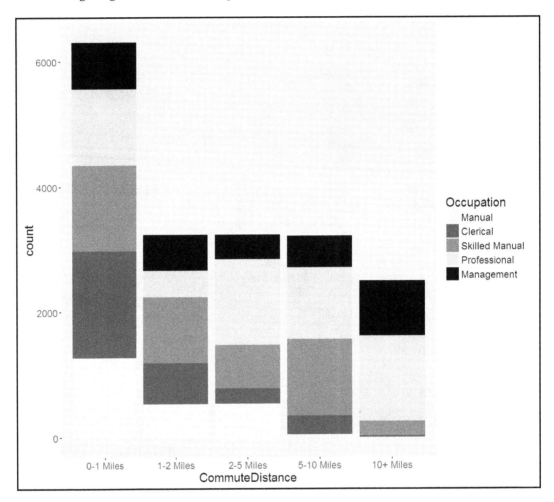

Figure 6.3: Occupation and CommuteDistance association

You probably already know that now the Python examples follow. Let me define the correct order of the values for commute distance and occupation:

```
# Define CommuteDistance as ordinal
TM['CommuteDistance'] = TM['CommuteDistance'].astype('category')
TM['CommuteDistance'].cat.reorder_categories(
  ["0-1 Miles",
   "1-2 Miles","2-5 Miles",
   "5-10 Miles", "10+ Miles"], inplace=True)
# Define Occupation as ordinal
TM['Occupation'] = TM['Occupation'].astype('category')
TM['Occupation'].cat.reorder_categories(
  ["Manual",
   "Clerical","Skilled Manual",
   "Professional", "Management"], inplace=True)
```

Next, I can cross-tabulate the two variables with the pandas `crosstab()` function:

```
cdo = pd.crosstab(TM.Occupation, TM.CommuteDistance)
cdo
```

The result is the same as from the cross-tabulation in R. Now, I can calculate the chi-squared value, the degrees of freedom, and the probability, or the p-value, with the `chi2_contingency()` function from the `scipy` library:

```
from scipy.stats import chi2_contingency
chi2, p, dof, expected = chi2_contingency(cdo)
chi2
dof
p
```

The Python results are as follows:

```
chi2 4587.6766118547503
dof  16
p    0.0
```

Of course, the results are the same as in R. Note that the `chi2_contingency()` function also returns the expected frequencies, which I am not showing here.

Discovering associations between continuous and discrete variables

The last possibility left for discovering and measuring the strength of associations is dependencies between continuous and discrete variables. Let me start by an example. In the dataset I use, the `dbo.vTargetMail` view from the `AdventureWorksDW2017` demo database, I have the variables that show the occupation and the income of each person. You would expect that there is some association between these two variables—some occupations have higher mean and median income, some lower. However, there could be a surprise hidden in the data. Imagine that somebody would mark their occupation as `skilled manual` for an excellent basketball player, for an NBA star. By comparing the mean income over occupation, you could wrongly conclude that you need to go for a skilled manual job, to have the highest possible income. But the difference in mean income between skilled manual and other occupation comes in this case from the variability within the skilled manual group, and not from the variability of income between the groups. Therefore, we need to know how to measure these two variabilities and compare them, to get a more realistic insight of the data.

I usually start with T-SQL, then switch to R, and then to Python. This time, I want to start with a graphical presentation of differences of the means of a continuous variables in classes of a discrete variable. I am starting with Python. The following code creates a graph called a boxplot that analyzes income in classes of education:

```
sns.boxplot(x = 'Occupation', y = 'Income',
 data = TM)
plt.show()
```

Here is the graph created with the previous code:

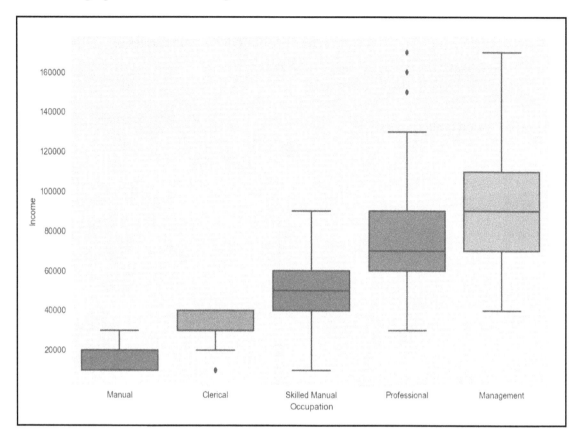

Figure 6.4: Boxplot for income in classes of occupation

The middle line in the last three boxes represents the median of the income in the specific class of occupation. For the left two classes, the median probably coincides with one of the box horizontal border lines. The top border of each box is the value in the third quartile position, and the bottom border is the value in the first quartile position. The height of a box shows you the inter-quartile range. The horizontal lines above and below each box, which are connected with vertical lines with the borders of the boxes, are the estimated limits of the regular values. These horizontal lines are also called the fences, or whiskers. By default, they are positioned at one-and-a-half times the IQR above or below the boxes' borders. The dots outside the fences are potential outliers.

Another nice presentation of a distribution of a continuous variable in classes of a discrete one is a `violinplot`. It tells you all of the information of a boxplot, and, in addition, it shows also the shape of the distribution of the continuous variable in classes of the discrete variable. The following violinplot shows the distribution of age in classes of occupation:

```
sns.violinplot(x = 'Occupation', y = 'Age',
 data = TM, kind = 'box', size = 8)
plt.show()
```

The graph created is shown here:

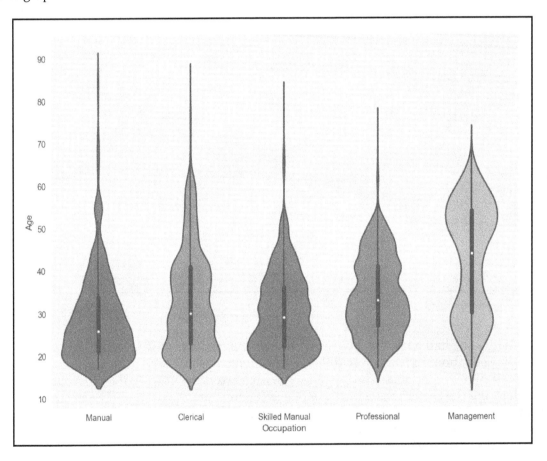

Figure 6.5: A violinplot of age in classes of occupation

You can find more examples in the additional code associated with this chapter. For now, let's switch from graphs to numbers, and from Python to T-SQL. I will introduce the statistical method called **analysis of variance**, or **ANOVA**. I am introducing here a quite simple, but useful, version of this analysis, also called a **one-way ANOVA**.

I need to calculate the variance between groups, usually denoted as MS_A. It is defined as the sum of squares of deviations of the group means from the total mean, and then multiplied by the number of elements, or cases, in each group. The degrees-of-freedom number is equal to the number of groups, usually marked with the letter a, minus one. Here is the formula:

$$MS_A = SS_A/DF_A; SS_A = \sum_{i=1}^{a} n_i * (\mu_i - \mu)^2; DF_A = (a - 1)$$

These are the meanings of the formula elements:

- MS_A is the variance between groups.
- SS_A is the sum of squares of deviations of the group means from the total mean.
- DF_A is the number of the degrees of freedom between groups.
- n_i is the number of cases in the ith group.
- a is the number of groups.
- μ is the overall mean.
- μ_i is the mean in the ith group of the discrete variable.
- The variance within groups MS_E is calculated with the sum of squares of deviations of individual values from the group mean. The next step is to summarize these squares over all groups. The degrees of freedom for each group is the number of cases in each group minus one, and the total degrees of freedom number is the sum of groups' degrees of freedom. Here is this quite complex formula:

$$MS_E = SS_E/DF_E; SS_E = \sum_{i=1}^{a} \sum_{j=1}^{n_i} (v_{ij} - \mu_i)^2; DF_E = \sum_{i=1}^{a} (n_i - 1)$$

The meanings of the formula elements are as follows:

- MS_E is the variance within groups
- SS_A is the sum of squares of deviations within groups

- DF_E is the sum of degrees of freedom within groups
- a is the number of groups
- n_i is the number of cases in the ith group
- v_{ij} is the value of the variable of the jth case in the ith group
- μ_i is the mean in the ith group of the discrete variable

After you have these calculations, you can calculate the **F ratio** with the following formula:

$$F = MS_A/MS_E$$

The *F* value tells you whether the two variables are associated. If they are, then the difference of the means of the continuous variable in groups of the discrete variable comes from the difference between groups, otherwise from the difference within groups. You can read the significance and the probability for the *F* value and the degrees of freedom you calculate from the F value tables, or from free web calculators. Here, again, is just an example of a site where you can check the F value you get: http://www.socscistatistics. com/pvalues/fdistribution.aspx. And, here is the T-SQL code that calculates all of the values just explained:

```
WITH Anova_CTE AS
(
SELECT EnglishOccupation, Age,
 COUNT(*) OVER (PARTITION BY EnglishOccupation) AS gr_CasesCount,
 DENSE_RANK() OVER (ORDER BY EnglishOccupation) AS gr_DenseRank,
 SQUARE(AVG(Age) OVER (PARTITION BY EnglishOccupation) -
 AVG(Age) OVER ()) AS between_gr_SS,
 SQUARE(Age -
 AVG(Age) OVER (PARTITION BY EnglishOccupation))
 AS within_gr_SS
FROM dbo.vTargetMail
)
SELECT N'Between groups' AS [Source of Variation],
 SUM(between_gr_SS) AS SS,
 (MAX(gr_DenseRank) - 1) AS df,
 SUM(between_gr_SS) / (MAX(gr_DenseRank) - 1) AS MS,
 (SUM(between_gr_SS) / (MAX(gr_DenseRank) - 1)) /
 (SUM(within_gr_SS) / (COUNT(*) - MAX(gr_DenseRank))) AS F
FROM Anova_CTE
UNION
SELECT N'Within groups' AS [Source of Variation],
 SUM(within_gr_SS) AS SS,
```

```
(COUNT(*) - MAX(gr_DenseRank)) AS df,
SUM(within_gr_SS) / (COUNT(*) - MAX(gr_DenseRank)) AS MS,
NULL AS F
FROM Anova_CTE;
```

The result of this code is as follows:

```
Source of Variation SS      df     MS F
------------------- ------- ----- ---------------- ----------------------
Between groups      333932  4      83483            732.90193767293
Within groups       2104896 18479 113.907462525028 NULL
```

If you use the site I mentioned, you can see that this is quite a large F value, significant at a level lower than 0.01, meaning that you can safely reject the null hypothesis and say that age and occupation are associated.

It's time to switch to R. The code in R is much shorter than the code in T-SQL. I am showing first the mean of the income in groups of the commute distance, then making the analysis of the variance with the aov() function from the base installation, and then displaying the results:

```
aggregate(TM$Income, by = list(TM$CommuteDistance), FUN = mean)
AssocTest <- aov(TM$Income ~ TM$CommuteDistance)
summary(AssocTest)
```

Here are the results of the R code:

```
   Group.1      x
1 0-1 Miles  49660.86
2 1-2 Miles  50043.32
3 2-5 Miles  57857.14
4 5-10 Miles 62380.21
5 10+ Miles  78805.13
                    Df    Sum Sq    Mean Sq   F value Pr(>F)
TM$CommuteDistance  4     1.776e+12 4.439e+11 469     <2e-16 ***
Residuals           18479 1.749e+13 9.465e+08
```

You can see that the income is also associated with the commute distance. Apparently, people with higher incomes live in suburbs, quite far away from the place where they work. You can see this also in the following diagram, for which I use the plotmeans() function from the gplots package. This package is usually pre-installed, so you should install it only in case you don't have it yet:

```
# install.packages("gplots")
library(gplots)
plotmeans(TM$Income ~ TM$CommuteDistance,
  bars = TRUE, p = 0.99, barwidth = 3,
```

```
col = "red", lwd = 3,
main = "Yearly Income in Groups",
ylab = "Yearly Income",
xlab = "Commute Distance")
```

Here is the graph:

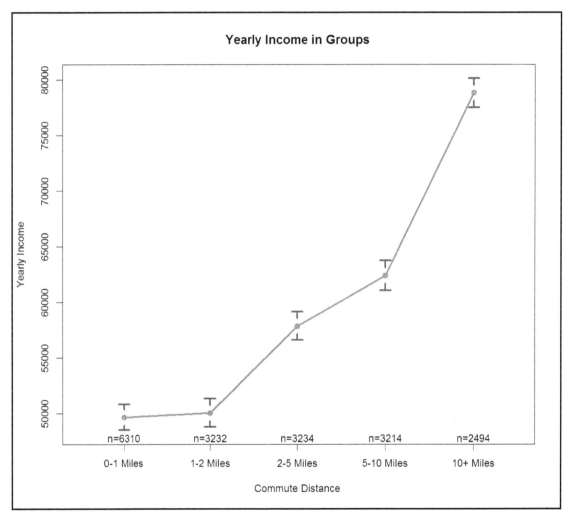

Figure 6.6: The means of the income in groups of the commute distance

The next step is to express an association with a formula, where you define a dependent variable as a function of one or more independent ones. I will show you the linear regression formula calculation in the last sector of this chapter.

Expressing dependencies with a linear regression formula

The simplest **linear regression** formula for two continuous variables is as follows:

$$Y = a + bX$$

The slope for this linear function is denoted with b and the intercept with a. When calculating these values, you try to find the line that fits the data points the best, where the deviations from the line are the smallest. The formula for the slope is as follows:

$$Slope(Y) = (\sum_{i=1}^{n}(X_i - \mu(X)) * (Y_i - \mu(Y)))/(\sum_{i=1}^{n}(X_i - \mu(X))^2)$$

Once you have the slope, it is easy to calculate the intercept, as shown here:

$$Intercept(Y) = \mu(Y) - Slope(Y) * \mu(X)$$

The decision regarding which variable is dependent and which independent is up to you. Of course, this also depends on the problem you are trying to solve, and on common sense. For example, you would probably not model gender as a dependent variable of income, but would do the opposite. The formulas don't tell you that. You actually calculate two formulas, name the first regression line and the second regression line, with both variables playing a different role in each equation.

Here is the calculation of both slopes and both intercepts for the number of cars owned and the yearly income variables:

```
WITH CoVarCTE AS
(
SELECT 1.0*NumberCarsOwned as val1,
 AVG(1.0*NumberCarsOwned) OVER () AS mean1,
 1.0*YearlyIncome AS val2,
 AVG(1.0*YearlyIncome) OVER() AS mean2
FROM dbo.vTargetMail
)
SELECT Slope1=
 SUM((val1 - mean1) * (val2 - mean2))
 /SUM(SQUARE((val1 - mean1))),
 Intercept1=
 MIN(mean2) - MIN(mean1) *
 (SUM((val1 - mean1)*(val2 - mean2))
```

```
      /SUM(SQUARE((val1 - mean1)))),
      Slope2=
      SUM((val1 - mean1) * (val2 - mean2))
      /SUM(SQUARE((val2 - mean2))),
      Intercept2=
      MIN(mean1) - MIN(mean2) *
      (SUM((val1 - mean1)*(val2 - mean2))
      /SUM(SQUARE((val2 - mean2))))
   FROM CoVarCTE;
```

The result is as follows:

```
Slope1            Intercept1        Slope2               Intercept2
---------------- ----------------- -------------------- --------------------
--
13234.5218173496 37418.1958624597 1.64539065625099E-05 0.55980108378968
```

The second part is where you express the number of cars as a linear function of income. In Python, the code for the same calculation is much shorter:

```
# Import linear regression
from sklearn.linear_model import LinearRegression
# Hyperparameters
model = LinearRegression(fit_intercept = True)
# Arrange the data - feature matrix and target vector (y is already vector)
X = TM[['Income']]
y = TM.NumberCarsOwned
# Fit the model to the data
model.fit(X, y)
# Slope and intercept
model.coef_; model.intercept_
```

The code imports the `LinearRegression()` function from the `sklearn` library. Then, it defines so-called **hyperparameters** for the model, or the general parameters for the calculation. In this case, the `fit_intercept = True` hyperparameter means that you want to calculate intercept as well, and not just the slope. You feed this function with a data frame that consists of independent variables, which is called a feature matrix, and a vector with the dependent variable, also called the target vector. The feature matrix consists in my case of a single variable, the `Income` variable. Then, you start the calculation, or fitting the model, with the `fit()` method of the model. Finally, I am showing the results:

```
1.64539066e-05
0.55980112596358134
```

Once you have the formula, you can make the predictions on new data. We will deal more with predictions and evaluating the models in `Chapter 8`, *Supervised Machine Learning*, of this book. Here is just a quick example of doing predictions in Python on the same dataset used for fitting the model, which is generally not a good practice. Then, I add the predictions to the dataset and show the actual and the predicted values for five random cases:

```
# Predictions
ypred = TM[['Income']]
yfit = model.predict(ypred)
TM['CarsPredicted'] = yfit
# Results
TM[['CustomerKey', 'NumberCarsOwned', 'CarsPredicted']].sample(5)
```

Here are the results. Note that you might get slightly different numbers:

```
     CustomerKey NumberCarsOwned CarsPredicted
2223 13223       1               1.711575
9694 20694       2               1.547036
6371 17371       2               1.217957
4364 15364       3               2.040653
1269 12269       0               1.053418
```

From the Python code, you can see that you can feed the `LinearRegression()` function with multiple input, or independent variables. You use a **multiple linear regression** formula. However, you can make things even more complex. You can use some independent variable in the regression equation as an nth order polynomial. This way, you get a **polynomial regression**. Many times, the relationship between two variables is not just simply linear. If you remember from the first section of this chapter, the correlation between age and income in my dataset is surprisingly low. What if the relationship is not linear? Let me show this relationship in a diagram.

In the following R code, I am randomly selecting 100 rows from my dataset. Then, I use the `ggplot()` function to create a scatterplot. I am adding the linear regression line in the plot, and the smoothed, or the polynomial, line:

```
TMSample <- TM[sample(nrow(TM), 100), c("Income", "Age")];
ggplot(data = TMSample, aes(x = Age, y = Income)) +
  geom_point() +
  geom_smooth(method = "lm", color = "red") +
  geom_smooth(color = "blue")
```

Here is the diagram. Please note that because the sample is random, you might get a slightly different diagram:

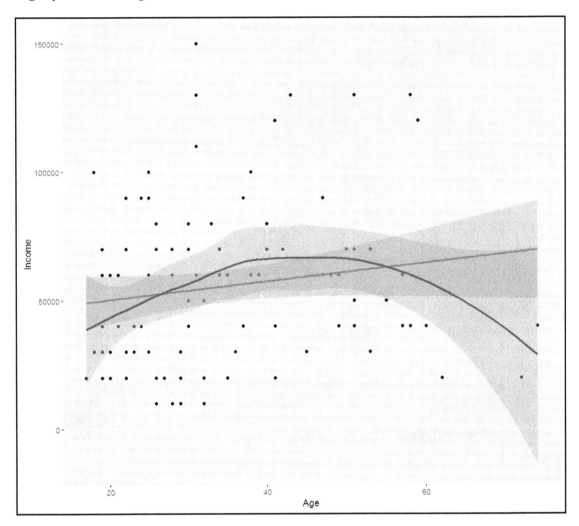

Figure 6.7: Income and age relationship

You can immediately see that the smoothed line fits data better than the straight line.

In R, you can use the `lm()` function from the base installation to find the linear regression formula coefficients. In the following code, I am expressing income as a polynomial function of age, using the `Age` variable in the formula once on the second and once on the first degree:

```
lrPoly <- lm(TM$Income ~ TM$Age + I(TM$Age ^ 2));
summary(lrPoly);
```

I am showing just the partial results of the `lm()` function here, just the coefficients:

```
Coefficients:
              Estimate
(Intercept) -1823.705
TM$Age       3094.791
I(TM$Age^2)  -35.608
```

You can interpret the result, as the income rises quite quickly with the age on the first degree, and decreases with the age on the second degree. Because with a higher age, the second part, the age on the second degree, starts to raise much quicker than the age on the first degree; the income starts to decrease at some age.

You could also make predictions in R, and compare the results with those from Python. You could try to add age on the third degree in the formula. You could create many additional models. Then, you would need to measure the quality of the predictions of the models, to select the best one for using it in production. As I already mentioned, I am going to show you how to evaluate predictive models in `Chapter 8`, *Supervised Machine Learning, of this book.*

Summary

In this chapter, after getting on overview of the data and finishing with the data preparation, you learned a bit about more complex statistics, which I called intermediate-level statistics, for analyzing your data. You learned how to explore relationships between pairs of variables with different possible content: both continuous, both discrete, and one continuous and one discrete. You have also seen how you can express a dependent variable as a linear or polynomial function of one or more independent variables. You saw how you can use the formula for predictions, and you have also seen some advanced visualizations of the data.

In `Chapter 7`, *Unsupervised Machine Learning*, we will be moving away from the predictive models. We will discuss the most popular unsupervised, or undirected, data science algorithms, and how to create the models based on those algorithms in different languages.

Unsupervised Machine Learning

7

Finally, we are there—we are going to do some real data science now. In the last two chapters, I am going to introduce some of the most popular advanced data mining and machine learning algorithms. I will show you how to use them to get in-depth knowledge from your data.

The most common separation of the algorithms is separation into two groups: the unsupervised, or undirected, and the supervised, or directed algorithms. The unsupervised ones have no target variable. You just try to find some interesting patterns, for example, some distinctive groups of cases, in your data. Then you need to analyze the results to make the interpretation possible. Talking about groups of cases, or clusters – you don't know the labels of those clusters in advance. Once you determine them, you need to check the characteristics of input variables in the clusters in order to get an understanding of the meaning of the clusters.

Before starting with the advanced algorithms, I will make a quick detour. I will just show you how you can install additional R and Python packages on the server side, for ML Services (In-Database).

This chapter covers the following:

- Installing ML Services (In-Database) packages
- Performing market-basket analysis
- Finding clusters of similar cases
- Dimensionality-reduction with principal-component analysis
- Extracting underlying factors from variables

Installing ML services (In-Database) packages

Because of security, you cannot just call the `install.packages()` R function from the `sys.sp_exacute_external_script` system procedure on the server side. There are many other ways to do it. You can find the complete list of options for installing R packages in the article *Install new R packages on SQL Server* at `https://docs.microsoft.com/en-us/sql/advanced-analytics/r/install-additional-r-packages-on-sql-server?view=sql-server-2017`. I will just show one option here, the one I am using when writing this book. I have my SQL Server installed on a virtual machine, and I can enable a web connection for the machine. Then the process of installing an additional R package is simple. You just need to run the R console, `R.exe`, from the ML Services (In-Database) installation, which is located in the `C:\Program Files\Microsoft SQL Server\MSSQL14.MSSQLSERVER\R_SERVICES\bin` folder for the default instance installation. You need to run `R.exe` as an administrator:

Running R.exe with administrative permissions

Before starting to install a package, I check the installed packages with the following T-SQL code:

```
USE AdventureWorksDW2017;
EXECUTE sys.sp_execute_external_script
@language=N'R',
@script =
N'str(OutputDataSet);
instpack <- installed.packages();
NameOnly <- instpack[,1];
OutputDataSet <- as.data.frame(NameOnly);'
WITH RESULT SETS (
  ( PackageName nvarchar(20) )
);
GO
```

Initially, I had 57 packages installed. Then I used the `install.packages("dplyr")` command in `R.exe` to install the `dplyr` library. After installation, I closed the `R.exe` console with the `q()` function. Then I used the preceding T-SQL code to re-check the installed packages. This time the number was 65, and the `dplyr` package was among them.

For Python, the simplest installation is from Visual Studio 2017. Of course, you can find all possible options in the documentation as well, in the *Install new Python packages on SQL Server* article at `https://docs.microsoft.com/en-us/sql/advanced-analytics/python/install-additional-python-packages-on-sql-server?view=sql-server-2017`. In VS 2017, you just need to open the **Python Environments** window (by default, on the right side of the screen) for the Python installation you are going to modify, select the **Packages** option in the drop-down list, and then in the text box below the drop-down list write the name of the package you want to install. VS 2017 creates the Python installation command, the `pip install` command, for you.

You can see this process in the following screenshot, where I am installing the `cntk` package, the Microsoft Cognitive Toolkit package for Python:

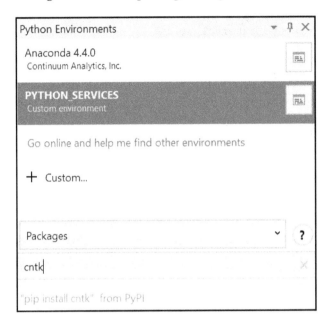

Installing a Python package

Again, before running the installation command, I check the number of Python packages installed with T-SQL:

```
EXECUTE sys.sp_execute_external_script
 @language = N'Python',
 @script = N'
import pip
import pandas as pd
instpack = pip.get_installed_distributions()
instpacksort = sorted(["%s==%s" % (i.key, i.version)
 for i in instpack])
dfPackages = pd.DataFrame(instpacksort)
OutputDataSet = dfPackages'
WITH RESULT SETS (
 ( PackageNameVersion nvarchar (150) )
);
GO
```

I had 128 packages installed initially, and 129 after I ran the `pip install` command.

Performing market-basket analysis

Market-basket analysis means, in its simplest implementation, finding which products tend to get purchased together, in the same basket. The basket might be either physical, such as a basket in a retail store, or a virtual one, such as a single Web order with one or more items. In the `AdventureWorksDW2017` demo database, there is a `dbo.vAssocSeqLineItems` view with the web purchase transactions with the content that I am examining with the following query:

```
SELECT TOP 3 *
FROM dbo.vAssocSeqLineItems;
```

The result is this:

```
OrderNumber LineNumber Model
----------- ---------- ------------
SO61313     1          Road-350-W
SO61313     2          Cycling Cap
SO61313     3          Sport-100
```

The `OrderNumber` column defines the basket, and the `Model` column identifies a single product in the basket. Note that I did not include the `ORDER BY` clause in the query; therefore, you might get a different three rows than I did.

The first analysis is the counts of individual **items** and groups of items in a single basket, or **itemsets**. After you find popular itemsets, you can express the **association rules**, for example *if a customer purchases a road bike, they will purchase a cycling cap as well*. The count of an itemset is called the **support** for a rule. You can define some other measures:

- **Confidence**: The support for the combination divided by the support for the condition of a rule. For example, the *If a customer purchases road bike, then they will purchase cycling cap* rule can have a support of 80 for the itemset road bike, cycling cap, and a support of 100 for the condition, for the item road bike. This gives us a confidence of 80%.

- **Expected confidence**: The support for the consequence in the rule divided by the total number of transactions.

- **Lift**: The result of the division of the confidence with the expected confidence. Lift gives you the factor for which the probability of an itemset exceeds the probability of the same itemset when the items would be independent.

You can calculate the support for a single item with a very simple query:

```
SELECT Model, COUNT(*) AS Support
FROM dbo.vAssocSeqLineItems
GROUP BY Model
ORDER BY Support DESC;
```

The query also orders the results based on the popularity of the items. Here are the most popular items:

```
Model         Support
------------  -------
Sport-100     3782
Water Bottle  2489
Patch kit     1830
```

For two items itemsets, you can use the CROSS APPLY operator to find the combinations:

```
WITH Pairs_CTE AS
(
SELECT t1.OrderNumber,
 t1.Model AS Model1,
 t2.Model2
FROM dbo.vAssocSeqLineItems AS t1
 CROSS APPLY
 (SELECT Model AS Model2
 FROM dbo.vAssocSeqLineItems
 WHERE OrderNumber = t1.OrderNumber
 AND Model > t1.Model) AS t2
)
SELECT Model1, Model2, COUNT(*) AS Support
FROM Pairs_CTE
GROUP BY Model1, Model2
ORDER BY Support DESC;
```

Here are the three most popular pairs of items:

```
Model1               Model2        Support
-------------------- ------------  -------
Mountain Bottle Cage Water Bottle  993
Road Bottle Cage     Water Bottle  892
Mountain Tire Tube   Sport-100     747
```

For itemsets that consist of three items, add another CROSS APPLY:

```
WITH Pairs_CTE AS
(
SELECT t1.OrderNumber,
 t1.Model AS Model1,
 t2.Model2
FROM dbo.vAssocSeqLineItems AS t1
 CROSS APPLY
 (SELECT Model AS Model2
 FROM dbo.vAssocSeqLineItems
 WHERE OrderNumber = t1.OrderNumber
 AND Model > t1.Model) AS t2
),
Triples_CTE AS
(
SELECT t2.OrderNumber,
 t2.Model1,
 t2.Model2,
 t3.Model3
FROM Pairs_CTE AS t2
 CROSS APPLY
 (SELECT Model AS Model3
 FROM dbo.vAssocSeqLineItems
 WHERE OrderNumber = t2.OrderNumber
 AND Model > t2.Model1
 AND Model > t2.Model2) AS t3
)
SELECT Model1, Model2, Model3, COUNT(*) AS Support
FROM Triples_CTE
GROUP BY Model1, Model2, Model3
ORDER BY Support DESC;
```

Here are the top three results:

```
Model1               Model2        Model3        Support
-------------------- ------------- ------------- -------
Mountain Bottle Cage Mountain-200  Water Bottle  343
Mountain Bottle Cage Sport-100     Water Bottle  281
Road Bottle Cage     Road-750      Water Bottle  278
```

You can notice that the queries are becoming more and more complex. It's time to switch to R. You can find the **association rules** algorithm in the arules package. The following code installs the package, if needed, and then loads the necessary libraries and reads the data from SQL Server:

```
# install.packages("arules")
library(arules)
```

```
library(RODBC)
con <- odbcConnect("AWDW", uid = "RUser", pwd = "Pa$$w0rd")
df_AR <- as.data.frame(sqlQuery(con,
 "SELECT OrderNumber, Model
 FROM dbo.vAssocSeqLineItems
 ORDER BY OrderNumber, Model;"
), stringsAsFactors = FALSE)
close(con)
```

The next step is to define the transactions and the items. I am also inspecting the transactions in the same code block:

```
# Defining transactions
trans <- as(split(df_AR[, "Model"],
 df_AR[, "OrderNumber"]),
 "transactions")
# Transactions info
inspect(trans[6:8])
```

Here are three transactions:

```
    items                                        transactionID
[1] {Fender Set - Mountain,Sport-100}            SO61318
[2] {LL Road Tire,Patch kit,Road Tire Tube}      SO61319
[3] {Mountain Bottle Cage,Sport-100,Water Bottle} SO61320
```

Now I can use the `apriori()` function to extract the rules. I use some parameters in the function to extract only the rules with itemsets with two items or more, and to extract only the rules that exceed the minimal support and minimal confidence:

```
AR <- apriori(trans,
 parameter = list
 (minlen = 2,
 supp = 0.03,
 conf = 0.05,
 target = "rules"))
inspect(AR, ruleSep = "---->", itemSep = " + ")
```

Here is the output for the first three rules:

```
    lhs                    rhs                  support    confidence
lift
[1] {ML Mountain Tire}  ----> {Mountain Tire Tube} 0.03321544  0.6565350
4.8079356
[2] {Mountain Tire Tube} ----> {ML Mountain Tire}   0.03321544  0.2432432
4.8079356
[3] {Touring Tire}      ----> {Touring Tire Tube}  0.03890512  0.8709122
12.6559602
```

You can sort the output based on any of the terms, the support, the confidence, or the lift, to find the rules that are most interesting to your business. There is also a very nice graphical representation of the association rules possible with the `arulesViz` package, as the following code shows:

```
# install.packages("arulesViz")
library(arulesViz)
# Rules graph
plot(AR, method = "graph", control = list(type = "items"))
```

The following screenshot shows the rules graph:

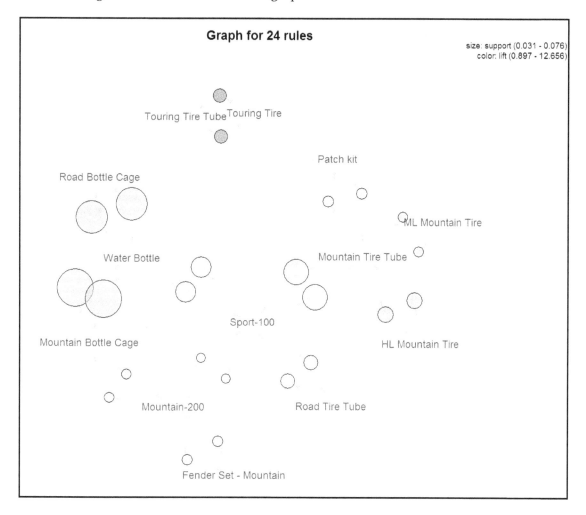

Association rules graph

Of course, it is possible to find the association rules in Python as well. However, for the sake of brevity, I am only pointing you to a very useful library called `Orange`, specifically to the association-rules module at `https://orange.readthedocs.io/en/latest/reference/rst/Orange.associate.html`. Don't worry; there will be more Python code later.

Finding clusters of similar cases

With **cluster analysis**, you try to find specific groups of cases, based on the **similarity** of the input variables. These groups, or clusters, help you understand your cases, for example, your customers or your employees. The clustering process groups the data based on the values of the variables, so the cases within a cluster have high similarity; however, these cases are very dissimilar to cases in other clusters. Similarity can be measured with different measures. Geometric distance is an example of a measure for similarity. You define an n-dimensional hyperspace, where each input variable defines one dimension, or one axis. Values of the variables define points in this hyperspace; these points are, of course, the cases. Now you can measure the geometric distance of each case from all other cases.

There are many different clustering algorithms. The most popular one is the **K-means** algorithm. With this algorithm, you define the number of K clusters in advance. The algorithm tries to find the K mean locations, or **centroids**, of the K groups; therefore, you can see where the name came from. The K-means algorithm assigns each case to exactly one cluster, to the closest centroid.

I will use the scalable `rxKmeans()` function from the Microsoft `RevoScaleR` package for the cluster analysis. As always, let's start by reading the data:

```
con <- odbcConnect("AWDW", uid = "RUser", pwd = "Pa$$w0rd")
TM <-
 sqlQuery(con,
 "SELECT CustomerKey, CommuteDistance,
 TotalChildren, NumberChildrenAtHome,
 Gender, HouseOwnerFlag,
 NumberCarsOwned, MaritalStatus,
 Age, BikeBuyer, Region,
 YearlyIncome AS Income,
 EnglishEducation AS Education,
 EnglishOccupation AS Occupation
 FROM dbo.vTargetMail")
close(con)
```

The `rxKmeans()` function accepts numeric data only. I want to use the Education variable as an input variable as well. I will create an additional integer variable from it, where the numbers order will follow the order of the levels of this factor. Therefore, I have to define the order correctly:

```
# Order Education
TM$Education = factor(TM$Education, order = TRUE,
 levels = c("Partial High School",
 "High School", "Partial College",
 "Bachelors", "Graduate Degree"))
# Create integer Education
TM$EducationInt = as.integer(TM$Education)
```

Now I can load the `RevoScaleR` library and train the model:

```
library(RevoScaleR)
ThreeClust <- rxKmeans(formula = ~NumberCarsOwned + Income + Age +
 NumberChildrenAtHome + BikeBuyer + EducationInt,
 data = TM, numClusters = 3)
```

I got the clusters; however, at this time, I have no idea what they mean. To analyze the clusters, I am adding the clusters to the original data frame, as the 16th column with the name `ClusterID`. The values of this column can be 1, 2, or 3:

```
TMClust <- cbind(TM, ThreeClust$cluster)
names(TMClust)[16] <- "ClusterID"
```

Now I will do a graphical analysis in order to get an idea of what kind of customers the clusters represent. The next portion of code is quite long, although not overly complex. I am attaching the TM data frame to the search path, so I don't need to write all of the variables with the data frame name prefix. Then I divide the plotting area into a 2 x 2 matrix; I will show four graphs in a single area. Then I analyze the distribution of four different variables in the clusters with four different graphs. Finally, I restore the 1 x 1 plotting area and detach the data frame from the search path:

```
# Attach the new data frame
attach(TMClust);
# Saving parameters
oldpar <- par(no.readonly = TRUE);
# Defining a 2x2 graph
par(mfrow = c(2, 2));
# Income and clusters
boxplot(Income ~ ClusterID,
 main = "Yearly Income in Clusters",
 notch = TRUE,
 varwidth = TRUE,
 col = "orange",
```

```r
 ylab = "Yearly Income",
 xlab = "Cluster Id")
# BikeBuyer and clusters
nc <- table(BikeBuyer, ClusterID)
barplot(nc,
 main = 'Bike buyer and cluster ID',
 xlab = 'Cluster Id', ylab = 'BikeBuyer',
 legend = rownames(nc),
 col = c("blue", "yellow"),
 beside = TRUE)
# Education and clusters
nc <- table(Education, ClusterID)
barplot(nc,
 main = 'Education and cluster ID',
 xlab = 'Cluster Id', ylab = 'Total Children',
 col = c("black", "blue", "green", "red", "yellow"),
 beside = TRUE)
legend("topright", rownames(nc), cex = 0.6,
 fill = c("black", "blue", "green", "red", "yellow"))
# Age and clusters
boxplot(Age ~ ClusterID,
 main = "Age in Clusters",
 notch = TRUE,
 varwidth = TRUE,
 col = "Green",
 ylab = "Yearly Income",
 xlab = "Cluster Id")
# Clean up
par(oldpar)
detach(TMClust)
```

You can see the results of the code in the following screenshot:

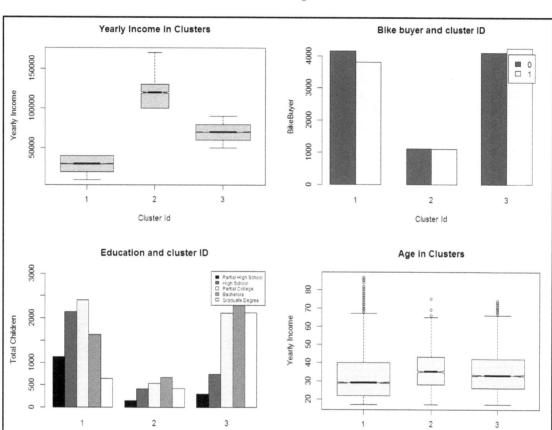

Analysis of clusters

You can see from the graphs that in cluster 1, there are younger people, who are less educated, with quite a low income. In cluster 2, there are slightly older people than in the other two clusters with a very high income. In cluster 3, medium-age professionals with quite high incomes prevail.

It would not be efficient to program the complete algorithm in T-SQL. However, I can use R code. I will prepare a temporary table for the results first:

```
CREATE TABLE #tmp
  (CustomerKey INT NOT NULL,
   NumberChildrenAtHome INT NOT NULL,
   NumberCarsOwned INT NOT NULL,
```

```
   Age INT NOT NULL,
   BikeBuyer INT NOT NULL,
   Income INT NOT NULL,
   ClusterID INT NOT NULL);
GO
```

The next step is to call the `sys.sp_execute_external_script` procedure in an `INSERT` statement. The procedure executes the R script that finds the clusters for me and returns a data frame with the original data and the cluster membership:

```
INSERT INTO #tmp
EXECUTE sys.sp_execute_external_script
 @language = N'R'
 ,@script = N'
 library(RevoScaleR)
 ThreeClust <- rxKmeans(formula = ~NumberCarsOwned + Income + Age +
 NumberChildrenAtHome + BikeBuyer,
 data = TM, numClusters = 3)
 TMClust <- cbind(TM, ThreeClust$cluster);
 names(TMClust)[7] <- "ClusterID";
 '
 ,@input_data_1 = N'
 SELECT CustomerKey, NumberChildrenAtHome,
 NumberCarsOwned, Age, BikeBuyer,
 YearlyIncome AS Income
 FROM dbo.vTargetMail;'
 ,@input_data_1_name = N'TM'
 ,@output_data_1_name = N'TMClust';
GO
```

Now I can analyze the clusters with T-SQL:

```
SELECT ClusterID, AVG(1.0*Income) AS AvgIncome
FROM #tmp
GROUP BY ClusterID
ORDER BY ClusterID;
```

Here are the results:

```
ClusterID AvgIncome
--------- -------------
1             68270.108043
2            120641.492265
3             28328.305681
```

Note that this time cluster 3 has the lowest income. Because the labels of the clusters are not known in advance, you can get different labels each time you execute the code.

Again, I am skipping Python in this section. However, I will start with Python in the next section, and show a clustering algorithm that will use the principal components found.

Principal components and factor analyses

The **principal component analysis** (**PCA**) is a well-known undirected method for reducing the number of variables used in further analyses. This is also called **dimensionality-reduction**. In some projects, you could have hundreds, maybe even thousands of input variables. Using all of them for can input to clustering algorithm could lead to enormous time needed to train the model. However, many of those input variables that might vary together, might have some association.

PCA starts again with the hyperspace, where each input variable defines one axis. PCA searches for a set of new axes, a set of new variables, which should be linearly uncorrelated, called the principal components. The principal components are calculated in such a way that the first one includes the largest possible variability of the whole input variable set, the second the second largest, and so on. The calculation of the principal components is derived from linear algebra. The principal components are actually the eigenvectors of the covariance matrix of input variables. The eigenvalues of these eigenvectors define the order of the principal components; the first one has the largest eigenvalue, the second the next largest, and so on. After you find the principal components, you can keep only the first few ones in further analysis. Of course, you lose some variability. However, by selecting the fist few principal components, the loss is minimized, while the dimensionality is reduced substantially.

As promised, I will finally use Python in this chapter. First, I need to import the necessary libraries and read the data:

```
# Imports
import numpy as np
import pandas as pd
import pyodbc
import matplotlib as mpl
import matplotlib.pyplot as plt
import seaborn as sns
# Reading the data from SQL Server
con = pyodbc.connect('DSN=AWDW;UID=RUser;PWD=Pa$$w0rd')
query = """SELECT CustomerKey, CommuteDistance,
 TotalChildren, NumberChildrenAtHome,
 Gender, HouseOwnerFlag,
 NumberCarsOwned, MaritalStatus,
 Age, BikeBuyer, Region,
 YearlyIncome AS Income,
```

```
EnglishEducation AS Education,
EnglishOccupation AS Occupation
FROM dbo.vTargetMail"""
TM = pd.read_sql(query, con)
```

In the next step, I have to import the PCA() function from the sklearn library and define the data frame with the input variables, or the feature matrix:

```
# Import PCA
from sklearn.decomposition import PCA
# Feature matrix
X = TM[["TotalChildren", "HouseOwnerFlag", "Age", "Income",
  "NumberChildrenAtHome", "NumberCarsOwned", "BikeBuyer"]]
```

In the next step, I define the model and train, or fit it. I am also calling the transform() method to get a two-dimensional array of the two principal components' values for each case:

```
model = PCA(n_components = 2)
model.fit(X)
X_2D = model.transform(X)
```

In the next step, I assign the principal components to the original data frame:

```
TM['PCA1'] = X_2D[:, 0]
TM['PCA2'] = X_2D[:, 1]
```

Now I can try to understand how the principal components are connected with the original variables. For example, I am using the seaborn lmplot() function to draw a scatterplot with regression lines of the NumberCarsOwned variable distribution in the plane defined with the two principal components:

```
ax = sns.lmplot('PCA1', 'PCA2', hue = 'NumberCarsOwned',
  data = TM, fit_reg = True, legend_out = False,
  palette = ("green", "red", "blue", "yellow", "black"),
  x_bins = 15, scatter_kws={"s": 100})
ax.set_xlabels(fontsize=16)
ax.set_ylabels(fontsize=16)
ax.set_xticklabels(fontsize=12)
ax.set_yticklabels(fontsize=12)
plt.show()
```

You can see the plot in the following screenshot:

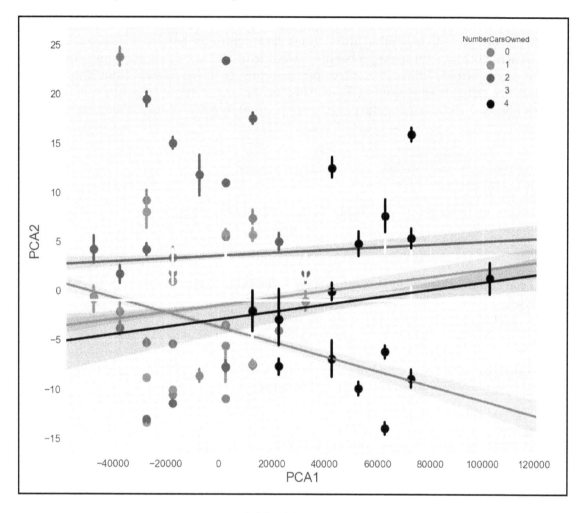

Analyzing principal components

I mentioned the main purpose of PCA is to use the first few principal components in further analysis. I will use the two principal components instead of the original variables to find three clusters again, this time with Python and with the **Gaussian mixture models** (**GMM**) algorithm. This algorithm also defines the K centroids; however, it assigns each case to each centroid with some probability by covering the cases with the Gaussian curves around each centroid. This is also called soft clustering, to differentiate it from K-means, which is also called hard clustering. I am using the `GaussianMixture()` function from the sklearn library. I am also using the `predict()` method to get the cluster membership vector:

```
# GMM clustering
from sklearn.mixture import GaussianMixture
# Define and train the model
X = TM[["PCA1", "PCA2"]]
model = GaussianMixture(n_components = 3, covariance_type = 'full')
model.fit(X)
# Get the clusters vector
y_gmm = model.predict(X)
```

Now I can add the cluster membership vector to the original data frame and check the first few cases:

```
TM['cluster'] = y_gmm
TM.head()
```

Before analyzing the distribution of other variables in the clusters, I am going to properly order the `CommuteDistance` and Occupation variables:

```
# Define CommuteDistance as ordinal
TM['CommuteDistance'] = TM['CommuteDistance'].astype('category')
TM['CommuteDistance'].cat.reorder_categories(
 ["0-1 Miles",
 "1-2 Miles","2-5 Miles",
 "5-10 Miles", "10+ Miles"], inplace=True)
# Define Occupation as ordinal
TM['Occupation'] = TM['Occupation'].astype('category')
TM['Occupation'].cat.reorder_categories(
 ["Manual",
 "Clerical","Skilled Manual",
 "Professional", "Management"], inplace=True)
```

Now I can create a nice graph for the commute distance distribution in clusters:

```
sns.countplot(x="CommuteDistance", hue="cluster", data=TM);
plt.show()
```

Here is the graph:

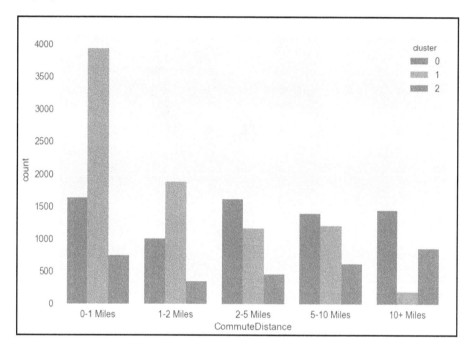

Commute distance distribution in clusters

I am continuing to analyze the Occupation variable:

```
sns.countplot(x="Occupation", hue="cluster", data=TM);
plt.show()
```

And here is the Occupation graph:

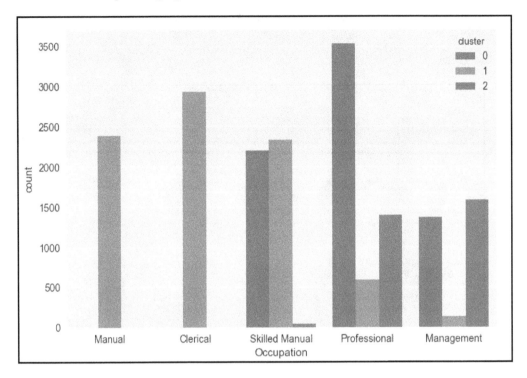

Occupation distribution in clusters

You can clearly see the difference in distribution of the two discrete variables in different clusters. Because now I have all variables, including the principal components and the cluster membership, in a single data frame, I can perform any analysis I want to.

Often, you don't need to understand the principal components you extract. However, you might want to find the underlying structure of variables, like you can find it for the cases with some kind of clustering. When you want to find the latent structure of the input variables, this is called **factor analysis (FA)**, or sometimes **exploratory factor analysis (EFA)**. The first principal components that are extracted, the **factors**, are used to explain the relationship of the input variables.

You can get a better understanding of the latent variable structure by rotating the new axes, the principal components, in the multidimensional hyperspace. With the **rotation**, you can maximize the correlation between principal components and different subsets of input variables. Therefore, one principal component becomes more associated with one subset of input variables, while another one with another subset.

From these associations, you can see what input variables the first few factors represent. The rotation can be **orthogonal** (the most known one is called **varimax**), preserving the orthogonality between the axes, or the factors. The rotation can also be **oblique** (a very well-known one is **promax**), which matches factors with specifics subsets even more, but also introduces some correlation between factors.

I am switching back to R. I will use the psych package—install it if needed and load it. In the following code, I will also be extracting the numerical variables only in the following code:

```
# install.packages("psych")
library(psych)
# Extracting numerical data only
TMFA <- TM[, c("TotalChildren", "NumberChildrenAtHome",
  "HouseOwnerFlag", "NumberCarsOwned",
  "BikeBuyer", "Income", "Age")]
```

Here is the code that extracts two factors by using an orthogonal rotation. The code then shows the results:

```
efaTM_varimax <- fa(TMFA, nfactors = 2, rotate = "varimax")
efaTM_varimax
```

I am showing just a small part of the results here. This part shows the correlation between the input variables and the two factors:

```
                       MR1    MR2
TotalChildren          0.36   0.75
NumberChildrenAtHome   0.77   0.18
HouseOwnerFlag         0.07   0.19
NumberCarsOwned        0.55   0.17
BikeBuyer             -0.07  -0.15
Income                 0.59   0.09
Age                   -0.05   0.68
```

Now let me repeat the factor analysis, this time with an oblique rotation:

```
efaTM_promax <- fa(TMFA, nfactors = 2, rotate = "promax")
efaTM_promax
```

The partial results are as follows:

```
                          MR1    MR2
TotalChildren            0.23   0.72
NumberChildrenAtHome     0.77   0.04
HouseOwnerFlag           0.03   0.19
NumberCarsOwned          0.55   0.07
BikeBuyer               -0.05  -0.14
Income                   0.60  -0.02
Age                     -0.19   0.72
```

You can see that with the oblique rotation, it is even more clear how the input variables are connected to the two factors. You can see these correlations, including the correlation between the two factors, with the help of the `fa.diagram()` function. I am showing diagrams for both rotations in the same graph:

```
par(mfrow = c(1, 2))
fa.diagram(efaTM_varimax, simple = FALSE,
  main = "EFA Varimax", cex = 1.2,
  e.size = .07, rsize = .12)
fa.diagram(efaTM_promax, simple = FALSE,
  main = "EFA Promax", cex = 1.3,
  e.size = .07, rsize = .12)
par(oldpar)
```

Here is the result of the previous code:

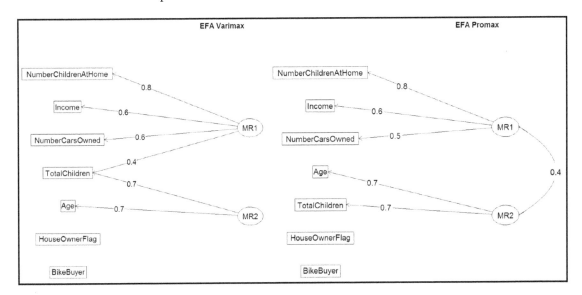

Correlations between factors and input variables

From this diagram, you can clearly see which input variables are represented with which factors. Note that with varimax rotation, the `TotalChildren` variables is correlated with both factors, while with promax rotation, the variables connected with each factor do not overlap. However, there is an association between both factors.

Summary

This chapter introduced the most popular unsupervised data-mining and machine-learning methods, including the association rules, the different types of clustering, the principal-component analysis, and the factor analysis. In addition, you learned how to add either R or Python packages to the ML services (In-Database). After warming up in the first three chapters, the complexity of the work and the analyses have increased. I have left the supervised methods, which are used for probably the most exciting part—predictive analytics—for the last chapter of this book.

8
Supervised Machine Learning

In `Chapter 6`, *Intermediate Statistics and Graphs*, we read about intermediate statistics with linear regression. I will continue this chapter from that point. Linear regression is already an algorithm you can use for predictions. You can make predictions with the directed, or the supervised, algorithms. Supervised algorithms have a target, or a dependent variable. They try to explain the values of that variable with the formula and the values of the independent variables. This explanation is stored in a model, which you use to predict the target variable value on a new dataset. The dependent variable supervises the development of the model. In a real project, you create many models, and then you deploy the one that suits your business needs the best. Therefore, you need to evaluate the models before the deployment.

In this chapter, I will explain the following:

- Evaluating predictive models
- Using the Naive Bayes algorithm
- Predicting with logistic regression
- Trees, forests, and more trees
- Predicting with T-SQL

Evaluating predictive models

To evaluate predictive models, you start by splitting your dataset into two disjunctive subsets: a **training set** and a **test set**. There is no strict rule about how to perform this division. You can start by using 70% of the data for training and 30% for testing. You train the model on the training set. After the model is trained, you use it on the test set to predict the values of the target variable. However, because the test set also consists of the data where the target variable value is known, you can measure how well a model predicts, and compare different models.

There are quite a few possible measures, which I will explain in the next few paragraphs. Note that you can also use the same data for training and for testing. Although typically you get predictions that are too good, better than with a separate test set, you can still compare different models.

Let me start with T-SQL code that selects 30% of the data from the `dbo.vTargetMail` view for the test set. The important part is to select the data randomly. In T-SQL, you can use the `CRYPT_GEN_RANDOM()` function to generate random numbers, which you can use to select random rows, as the following code shows:

```
USE AdventureWorksDW2017;
GO
-- Test set
SELECT TOP 30 PERCENT
 CustomerKey, CommuteDistance,
 TotalChildren, NumberChildrenAtHome,
 Gender, HouseOwnerFlag,
 NumberCarsOwned, MaritalStatus,
 Age, Region,
 YearlyIncome AS Income,
 EnglishEducation AS Education,
 EnglishOccupation AS Occupation,
 BikeBuyer, 2 AS TrainTest
 INTO dbo.TMTest
FROM dbo.vTargetMail
ORDER BY CAST(CRYPT_GEN_RANDOM(4) AS INT);
```

Now it is easy to select the remaining 70% of the rows for the training set with help of the `NOT EXISTS` filter:

```
-- Training set
SELECT
 CustomerKey, CommuteDistance,
 TotalChildren, NumberChildrenAtHome,
 Gender, HouseOwnerFlag,
 NumberCarsOwned, MaritalStatus,
 Age, Region,
 YearlyIncome AS Income,
 EnglishEducation AS Education,
 EnglishOccupation AS Occupation,
 BikeBuyer, 1 AS TrainTest
 INTO dbo.TMTrain
FROM dbo.vTargetMail AS v
WHERE NOT EXISTS
 (SELECT * FROM dbo.TMTest AS t
 WHERE v.CustomerKey = t.CustomerKey);
GO
```

There are many possibilities for doing the split in R and Python. I used T-SQL because I will use the same training set in both languages, in order to be able to compare the models between different languages as well.

Let's start with a simple example of the evaluation. I will use Python with the `revoscalepy` Microsoft scalable library to create a linear model. First, let's import the basic data science libraries and read the data:

```
import numpy as np
import pandas as pd
import pyodbc
import matplotlib as mpl
import matplotlib.pyplot as plt
import seaborn as sns
# Reading the data from SQL Server
con = pyodbc.connect('DSN=AWDW;UID=RUser;PWD=Pa$$w0rd')
query = """SELECT CustomerKey, CommuteDistance,
 TotalChildren, NumberChildrenAtHome,
 Gender, HouseOwnerFlag,
 NumberCarsOwned, MaritalStatus,
 Age, Region, Income,
 Education, Occupation,
 BikeBuyer, TrainTest
 FROM dbo.TMTrain
 UNION
 SELECT CustomerKey, CommuteDistance,
 TotalChildren, NumberChildrenAtHome,
 Gender, HouseOwnerFlag,
 NumberCarsOwned, MaritalStatus,
 Age, Region, Income,
 Education, Occupation,
 BikeBuyer, TrainTest
 FROM dbo.TMTEST
 """
TM = pd.read_sql(query, con)
```

Note that I unioned the training and the test set into a single one again. I will split the data later in R and Python using the TrainTest variable, which is the flag that defines the set membership for a case.

Linear regression uses numerical variables only. I have some categorical variables. Some of them are ordinals. Let's define them properly with the following code:

```
# Define Education as ordinal
TM['Education'] = TM['Education'].astype('category')
TM['Education'].cat.reorder_categories(
 ["Partial High School",
```

```
  "High School","Partial College",
  "Bachelors", "Graduate Degree"], inplace=True)
TM['Education']
# Define CommuteDistance as ordinal
TM['CommuteDistance'] = TM['CommuteDistance'].astype('category')
TM['CommuteDistance'].cat.reorder_categories(
  ["0-1 Miles",
  "1-2 Miles","2-5 Miles",
  "5-10 Miles", "10+ Miles"], inplace=True)
# Define Occupation as ordinal
TM['Occupation'] = TM['Occupation'].astype('category')
TM['Occupation'].cat.reorder_categories(
  ["Manual",
  "Clerical","Skilled Manual",
  "Professional", "Management"], inplace=True)
```

From ordinals, it is easy to create integers:

```
TM['EducationInt'] = TM['Education'].cat.codes
TM['CommuteDistanceInt'] = TM['CommuteDistance'].cat.codes
TM['OccupationInt'] = TM['Occupation'].cat.codes
```

Now I can import the `rx_lin_mod()` and `rx_predict()` functions from the `revoscalepy` package. Then I can create a linear model. In the model, I am expressing the `NumberCarsOwned` variable as a linear function of the `TotalChildren`, `NumberChildrenAtHome`, `BikeBuyer`, `Occupation`, `Education`, and `CommuteDistance` variables. Note that for the last three ordinal variables, I use the three integer versions I just created:

```
from revoscalepy import rx_lin_mod, rx_predict
linmod = rx_lin_mod(
  """NumberCarsOwned ~ TotalChildren + OccupationInt + NumberChildrenAtHome
+
  EducationInt + CommuteDistanceInt + BikeBuyer""",
  data = TM)
```

As you can see from the code, I used the whole dataset for the training process. This mean I will do the predictions on the same data I used for training. I will show how to use the separate training and test sets later. Let's do the predictions and show the first few:

```
TMPredict = rx_predict(linmod, data = TM, output_data = TM)
TMPredict[["NumberCarsOwned", "NumberCarsOwned_Pred"]].head(5)
```

Here is the result:

```
NumberCarsOwned NumberCarsOwned_Pred
0 0                   1.170255
1 1                   1.639562
2 1                   1.826767
3 1                   1.356994
4 4                   2.108748
```

At first glance, you might be disappointed with the predictions. However, please note that for the lower actual number of cars, also the predicted number is lower. Therefore, the shape of the distribution is preserved. If you normalize the predictions into the scale from 0 to 4, the numbers would be much closer to the original values. I can use the area chart to show you that the distribution shape is preserved:

```
TMPredict[["NumberCarsOwned", "NumberCarsOwned_Pred"]].head(20).plot(kind =
"area",
 color = ('green','orange'))
plt.show()
```

You can see the area graph in the following diagram:

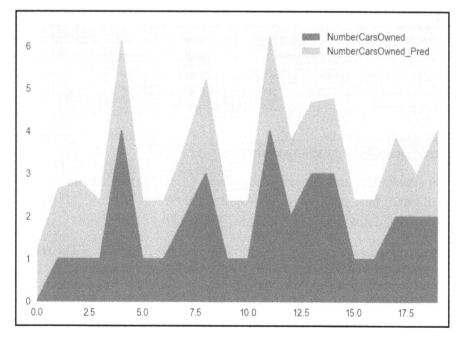

Area chart of original and predicted number of cars owned

Often, your target variable is discrete, with two possible values only, probably yes/no or true/false, showing some decision, or whether some action occurred. The most important way of showing the quality of the predictions is in the **classification matrix**, also called the **confusion matrix**. The following table shows the classification matrix:

	Predicted	Predicted
Actual	No	Yes
No	TN	FP
Yes	FN	TP

This is a 2 x 2 matrix (in the preceding table, there are also the headers for the rows and the columns). In the rows, there are the actual values, while the predicted values are in the columns. The confusion matrix values are written in bold and italics. In the top-left corner, there is the number of cases where the predicted value was no, and the actual value was no as well. These are **true negatives**. In the top-right corner, the prediction was yes, while the actual value was no. These are **false positives**. I hope you can see the logic of the matrix now and understand the meaning of the values in the bottom two cells: **false negatives** bottom-left, and **true positives** bottom-right.

Which of the four values from the matrix is the most important for you depends on a business problem. For example, for a marketing campaign, you might be mostly interested in true positives. For fraud-detection, besides true positives, you need to take special care about false positives as well. You probably don't want to cancel a credit card of your best customer because your model predicted incorrectly that the last transaction with this credit card was fraudulent. Now think of predicting areas of landslides. In this case, the false negatives play a big role. Imagine you predict there would be no landslide in some area, people build houses there, and then a landslide happens.

From the four values in the classification matrix, you can derive many other measures that combine them. Some of the most important are:

- Sensitivity, or recall, hit or rate, or true positive rate, defined as $TP / (TP + FN)$
- Fall-out or false positive rate, defined as $FN / (FN + TP)$
- Accuracy, defined as $(TP + TN) / (TP + TN + FP + FN)$

There are also some popular graphical presentations of the predictions. The **receiver operating characteristic** (**ROC**) curve plots the true-positive rate against the false-positive rate at various threshold settings. Such a curve is very useful for fraud-detection problems, for example. Another popular chart is the **lift chart**. In the lift chart, you can compare different models with random guessing. I will show concrete examples later in this chapter.

Using the Naive Bayes algorithm

The **Naive Bayes** algorithm is quite fast one, useful for the initial analysis of discrete variables. The algorithm calculates frequencies, or probabilities, for each possible state of every input variable in each state of the predictable variable. The probabilities are used for predictions on new datasets with known input attributes. As mentioned, the algorithm supports discrete (or discretized, of course) attributes only. Each input attribute is used separately from other input attributes. Therefore, input attributes are considered to be independent. I will show an example in Python. Let's start with the necessary imports:

```
from sklearn.metrics import accuracy_score
from sklearn.naive_bayes import GaussianNB
```

The next step is to create the training and the test set from the SQL Server data I read earlier. In addition, as with other algorithms from the `sklearn` library, I need to prepare the feature matrix and the target vector:

```
Xtrain = TM.loc[TM.TrainTest == 1,
  ['TotalChildren', 'NumberChildrenAtHome',
  'HouseOwnerFlag', 'NumberCarsOwned',
  'EducationInt', 'OccupationInt',
  'CommuteDistanceInt']]
ytrain = TM.loc[TM.TrainTest == 1, ['BikeBuyer']]
Xtest = TM.loc[TM.TrainTest == 2,
  ['TotalChildren', 'NumberChildrenAtHome',
  'HouseOwnerFlag', 'NumberCarsOwned',
  'EducationInt', 'OccupationInt',
  'CommuteDistanceInt']]
ytest = TM.loc[TM.TrainTest == 2, ['BikeBuyer']]
```

Now let's initialize and train the model:

```
model = GaussianNB()
model.fit(Xtrain, ytrain)
```

After the model is trained, we can use it to predict the BikeBuyer variable in the test set. I am also showing the accuracy score, the measure I introduced it in the previous section of this chapter:

```
ymodel = model.predict(Xtest)
accuracy_score(ytest, ymodel)
```

Here is the result:

```
0.6034980165885323
```

This is not too good. The Naive Bayes algorithm is useful for the preliminary analysis, to check which variables could be useful for the input. You use it before you analyze the data with more complex algorithms, because it is fast. Let me add the actual and the predicted values of the `BikeBuyer` variable to the test set:

```
Xtest['BikeBuyer'] = ytest
Xtest['Predicted'] = ymodel
```

Now I can show you the classification matrix, with numbers and graphically:

```
cdbb = pd.crosstab(Xtest.BikeBuyer, Xtest.Predicted)
cdbb
cdbb.plot(kind = 'bar',
  fontsize = 14, legend = True,
  use_index = True, rot = 1)
plt.show()
```

Here are the numerical results. You can note that the true positives are quite high:

```
Predicted    0    1
BikeBuyer
0          1546 1255
1           944 1801
```

The following diagram shows the classification matrix with a bar chart:

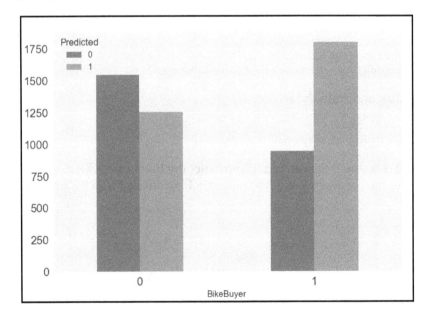

Classification matrix represented with a bar chart

Finally, I can analyze the distributions of input variables in classes of the actual and the predicted values for the `BikeBuyer` variable. First, here is a boxplot for the `TotalChildren` variable:

```
sns.boxplot(x = 'Predicted', y = 'TotalChildren',
  hue = 'BikeBuyer', data = Xtest,
  palette = ('red', 'lightgreen'))
plt.show()
```

This results in the following diagram:

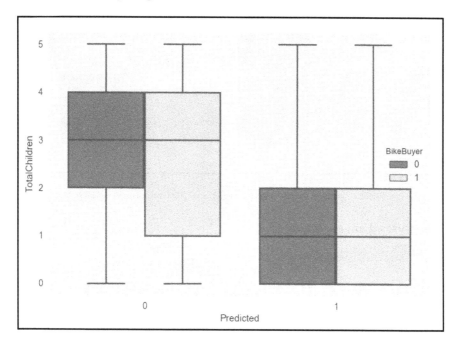

Analyzing TotalChildren in classes of the actual and predicted BikeBuyer variable

I will also make a boxplot for the `NumberCarsOwned` variable:

```
sns.barplot(x="Predicted", y="NumberCarsOwned",
  hue="BikeBuyer", data=Xtest,
  palette = ('yellow', 'blue'))
plt.show()
```

Here is the diagram:

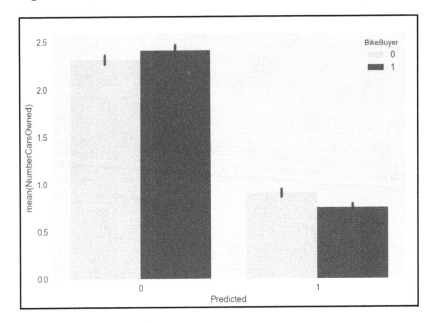

Figure 8.4: Analyzing NumberCyarsOwned in classes of the actual and predicted BikeBuyer variable

For the next analyses, I am switching to R.

Predicting with logistic regression

The next step is to do some analytics also in R. I will start with logistic regression. First, we need to read the data in R:

```
library(RODBC)
con <- odbcConnect("AWDW", uid = "RUser", pwd = "Pa$$w0rd")
TM <-
 sqlQuery(con,
 "SELECT CustomerKey, CommuteDistance,
 TotalChildren, NumberChildrenAtHome,
 Gender, HouseOwnerFlag,
 NumberCarsOwned, MaritalStatus,
 Age, Region, Income,
 Education, Occupation,
 BikeBuyer, TrainTest
 FROM dbo.TMTrain
 UNION
```

```
SELECT CustomerKey, CommuteDistance,
TotalChildren, NumberChildrenAtHome,
Gender, HouseOwnerFlag,
NumberCarsOwned, MaritalStatus,
Age, Region, Income,
Education, Occupation,
BikeBuyer, TrainTest
FROM dbo.TMTEST")
close(con)
```

The next step, similar to Python, is to define the factors and their levels accordingly:

```
# Define Education as ordinal
TM$Education = factor(TM$Education, order = TRUE,
 levels = c("Partial High School",
 "High School", "Partial College",
 "Bachelors", "Graduate Degree"))
# Define CommuteDistance as ordinal
TM$CommuteDistance = factor(TM$CommuteDistance, order = TRUE,
 levels = c("0-1 Miles",
 "1-2 Miles", "2-5 Miles",
 "5-10 Miles", "10+ Miles"))
# Define Occupation as ordinal
TM$Occupation = factor(TM$Occupation, order = TRUE,
 levels = c("Manual",
 "Clerical", "Skilled Manual",
 "Professional", "Management"))
```

Still not end of the preparation work. I need to define integers from ordinals:

```
TM$EducationInt = as.integer(TM$Education)
TM$CommuteDistanceInt = as.integer(TM$CommuteDistance)
TM$OccupationInt = as.integer(TM$Occupation)
```

I will also give the labels to the levels of the BikeBuyer factor variable:

```
TM$BikeBuyer <- factor(TM$BikeBuyer,
 levels = c(0, 1),
 labels = c("No", "Yes"))
```

I am splitting the data into the training and test sets:

```
TMTrain <- TM[TM$TrainTest == 1,]
TMTest <- TM[TM$TrainTest == 2,]
```

Now I am ready to introduce the **logistic regression** algorithm. In a logistic regression model, the input variables are called input units. The algorithm combines input values together into a single value. The combination can be done with a **weighted sum**. Then this single number is transformed into another number with the **logistic function**, also called the **sigmoid function**. The transformed value is the output unit. Both parts, the combination and the transformation with the weighted sum and the logistic function, together are called the **activation function**. The output value is the prediction. The logistic function returns values between zero and one. Values greater than 0.5 can be treated as a positive prediction, and lower as a negative prediction. Here is the formula for the sigmoid function:

$$S(x) = 1/(1 + e^{-x})$$

Logistic regression is quite popular. You can find the `glm()` function already in the base package. With the following code, I am training a model with `BikeBuyer` as the target variable and with only three input variables:

```
TMLogR <- glm(BikeBuyer ~
  Income + Age + NumberCarsOwned,
  data = TMTrain, family = binomial())
```

After the model is trained, I can use the `predict()` function to do the prediction. I am also discretizing the results into two values: yes and no. Then I create the confusion matrix:

```
probLR <- predict(TMLogR, TMTest, type = "response")
predLR <- factor(probLR > 0.5,
  levels = c(FALSE, TRUE),
  labels = c("No", "Yes"))
perfLR <- table(TMTest$BikeBuyer, predLR,
  dnn = c("Actual", "Predicted"))
perfLR
```

Here are the results. Compare this with the Naive Bayes algorithm results from the previous section:

```
          Predicted
Actual No    Yes
No      1769 1032
Yes     1173 1572
```

If you compared the results, you can see that the logistic regression outcome is better for true negatives, but worse for true positives. Let me include more input variables in the formula and test the model again:

```
TMLogR <- glm(BikeBuyer ~
```

```
   Income + Age + NumberCarsOwned +
   EducationInt + CommuteDistanceInt + OccupationInt,
   data = TMTrain, family = binomial())
 # Test the model
 probLR <- predict(TMLogR, TMTest, type = "response")
 predLR <- factor(probLR > 0.5,
   levels = c(FALSE, TRUE),
   labels = c("No", "Yes"))
 perfLR <- table(TMTest$BikeBuyer, predLR,
   dnn = c("Actual", "Predicted"))
 perfLR
```

Here are the results. They are only slightly better:

```
        Predicted
 Actual  No   Yes
 No      1784 1017
 Yes     1147 1598
```

Maybe it is time to try to analyze the data with another algorithm.

Trees, forests, and more trees

Probably the most popular classification and prediction algorithm is the **decision trees** algorithm. The algorithm gives quite good results and is easy to understand. The algorithm is also called **recursive partitioning**. You start with all the data in one group. Then you split the data with values of every single input variable, one by one. After each split, you check the distribution of the target variable in the new subgroups. You keep the split that gives you the purest subgroups in terms of the target variable and disregard all other splits. Then you split the subgroups again and again, until the purity of the target variable grows, or until some other stopping condition.

Decision trees use discrete variables. If some variables are continuous and the target variable is a continuous one as well, then you get the **regression trees**. Discrete variables are used for splits, and continuous variables for the regression formula in each branch of the tree. You get a **piecemeal linear regression**. Linear regression is just a simple regression tree without any split.

OK, that's enough of an introduction. Let's use the rpart() function from the base installation to grow the tree and immediately use it for predictions and for the classification matrix:

```
 TMRP <- rpart(BikeBuyer ~ MaritalStatus + Gender +
                  Education + Occupation +
```

```
              + NumberCarsOwned + TotalChildren +
              CommuteDistance + Region,
              data = TMTrain)
# Test the model
predDT <- predict(TMRP, TMTest, type = "class")
perfDT <- table(TMTest$BikeBuyer, predDT,
                dnn = c("Actual", "Predicted"))
perfDT
```

Here are the results:

```
          Predicted
Actual No    Yes
No      1678 1123
Yes      939 1806
```

The results are better than with any algorithm I used earlier. Before continuing with the analysis, let's draw the tree. I am using the prp() function from the rpart.plot package:

```
# install.packages("rpart.plot")
library(rpart.plot)
prp(TMRP, type = 2, extra = 104, fallen.leaves = FALSE);
```

You can see the tree in the following diagram:

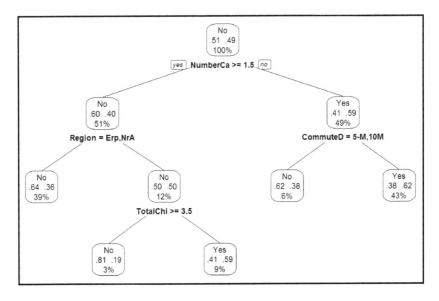

Decision tree for the BikeBuyer variable

Decision trees are implemented in many packages. A very popular version is the `ctree()` function from the `rpart` package:

```
# install.packages("party")
library(party)
TMDT <- ctree(BikeBuyer ~ MaritalStatus + Gender +
 Education + Occupation +
 NumberCarsOwned + TotalChildren +
 CommuteDistance + Region,
 data = TMTrain)
# Test the model
predDT <- predict(TMDT, TMTest, type = "response")
perfDT <- table(TMTest$BikeBuyer, predDT,
 dnn = c("Actual", "Predicted"))
perfDT
```

Here are the results of the `ctree()` function:

```
        Predicted
Actual No    Yes
No      2110  691
Yes      894 1851
```

You can see a substantial improvement. Especially the false positives are quite impressive compared to other models I made. Let me add the predictions to the test set and calculate the accuracy measure:

```
TMTest$Predicted <- predict(TMDT, newdata = TMTest)
# Calculate the overall accuracy.
TMTest$CorrectP <- TMTest$Predicted == TMTest$BikeBuyer
print(paste("Correct predictions: ",
 100 * mean(TMTest$CorrectP), "%"))
```

The accuracy is as follows:

```
Correct predictions: 71.4208438514245 %
```

This is a much better accuracy than I got with the Naive Bayes model. Because of the good ratio between true positives and false positives, I will draw the ROC curve for this model. First, I need to get the prediction probabilities, not just the predicted value. I can get them with the `treeresponse()` function and store them in the test data frame:

```
TMTest$Probabilities <-
 1 - unlist(treeresponse(TMDT, newdata = TMTest),
 use.names = F)[seq(1, nrow(TMTest) * 2, 2)]
```

Now I can use the ROCR library to get the version of the plot() function that can draw the ROC curve:

```
# install.packages("ROCR")
library(ROCR)
pred <- prediction(TMTest$Probabilities, TMTest$BikeBuyer)
perf <- performance(pred, "tpr", "fpr")
plot(perf, main = "ROC curve", colorize = T, cex.axis = 1.3, cex.lab = 1.4,
lwd = 6)
```

You can see the ROC curve in the following diagram:

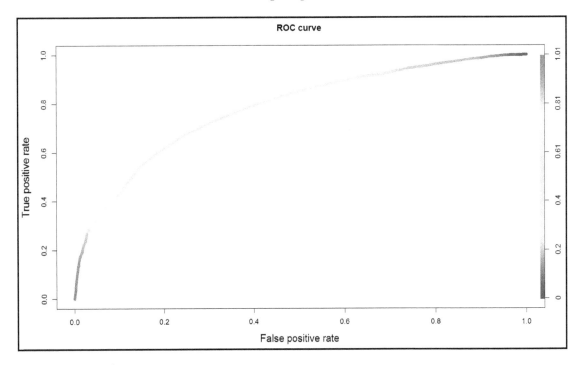

The ROC curve for the ctree() model

It seems as if the last model I created would be good for a fraud-detection problem. You could create ROC curves for other models as well and then compare them visually; the higher the curve, the better the model.

There are many additional versions of decision trees. The **random forests** algorithm builds many decision trees on the same training set, using random subsets from the training set. Then it averages the predictions from all of the models.

You can imagine that this algorithm is very resource-intensive. It can process multiple trees in parallel. I will use the scalable version of this algorithm built in the rxDForest() function of the RevoScaleR package. Here is the code:

```
library(RevoScaleR)
# Decision forest
rxDF <- rxDForest(BikeBuyer ~ CommuteDistance +
 NumberCarsOwned + Education,
 data = TMTrain, cp = 0.01)
# Test the model
predDF <- rxPredict(rxDF, data = TMTest, type = 'response')
TMDF <- cbind(TMTest['BikeBuyer'], predDF)
perfDF <- table(TMDF$BikeBuyer, TMDF$BikeBuyer_Pred,
 dnn = c("Actual", "Predicted"))
perfDF
```

The confusion matrix for this model is as follows:

```
        Predicted
Actual No   Yes
No     1874  927
Yes    1273 1472
```

You can see that the results are worse than with the previous model. However, please note that I used only a bunch of input variables. Anyway, this is how you work in a real project: you try different algorithms, with different inputs, and different parameters.

I will try another version of decision trees. The **gradient-boosting trees** also build many decision trees. However, they build one by one, serially. For each tree, the algorithm selects again a random subset of cases from the training set. However, in each step, it adds some cases for which the predictions were wrong in the previous step. This way, the algorithm lowers the false predictions. I am showing an example using the rxBTree() function from the RevoScaleR package:

```
rxBT <- rxBTrees(BikeBuyer ~ CommuteDistance +
 TotalChildren + NumberChildrenAtHome +
 Gender + HouseOwnerFlag +
 NumberCarsOwned + MaritalStatus +
 Age + Region + Income +
 Education + Occupation,
 data = TMTrain, cp = 0.01)
# Test the model
predBT <- rxPredict(rxBT, data = TMTest, type = 'response')
predBT['BBPredicted'] <- as.integer(predBT['BikeBuyer_prob'] >= 0.5)
TMBT <- cbind(TMTest['BikeBuyer'], predBT)
# Giving labels to BikeBuyer values
TMBT$BBPredicted <- factor(TMBT$BBPredicted,
```

```
  levels = c(0, 1),
  labels = c("No", "Yes"))
# View(predBT)
perfBT <- table(TMBT$BikeBuyer, TMBT$BBPredicted,
  dnn = c("Actual", "Predicted"))
perfBT
```

Note that this algorithm returns predictions in terms of probabilities, like the logistic regression. Therefore, in order to test the model, I had to add two intermediate steps: converting the probabilities to the numbers zero and one, and giving the labels to the numbers. Here are the results:

```
        Predicted
Actual No    Yes
No     1820  981
Yes    1134 1611
```

I will finish my modeling session now. For this example, I am declaring the rpart() function from the party package as the winner.

Predicting with T-SQL

The last question to answer is how you use the R and Python models in T-SQL. Of course, you can create the models and train them directly with the sys.sp_execute_external_script stored procedure. However, it would make no sense to retrain the complete model on the same training set for every new prediction, even if it is prediction on a single case. SQL Server 2017 introduces the PREDICT() function. Using this function means performing **native predictions** in SQL Server.

In order to use the PREDICT() function, you need to serialize the model in a SQL Server table, in a VARBINARY(MAX) column. You don't even have to have the ML Services (In-Database) installed in the SQL Server where you serialize your models to do the native predictions. The following code creates the table for the models:

```
CREATE TABLE dbo.dsModels
(Id INT NOT NULL IDENTITY(1,1) PRIMARY KEY,
 ModelName NVARCHAR(50) NOT NULL,
 Model VARBINARY(MAX) NOT NULL);
GO
```

Unfortunately, not all models are supported for native predictions, or for **real-time scoring**. Currently, in summer 2018, when I am writing this book, only some algorithms from the RevoScaleR and MicrosoftML libraries are supported.

However, the list of the supported algorithms is continuously growing. You can check the list of the supported algorithms in Microsoft Docs at `https://docs.microsoft.com/en-us/sql/advanced-analytics/real-time-scoring?view=sql-server-2017`.

The following code creates a decision tree model with the `rxDtrees()` function from the RevoScaleR package, and serializes the model in the table I just created:

```
DECLARE @model VARBINARY(MAX);
EXECUTE sys.sp_execute_external_script
 @language = N'R'
 ,@script = N'
 rxDT <- rxDTree(BikeBuyer ~ NumberCarsOwned +
 TotalChildren + Age + YearlyIncome,
 data = TM);
 model <- rxSerializeModel(rxDT, realtimeScoringOnly = TRUE);'
 ,@input_data_1 = N'
 SELECT CustomerKey, NumberCarsOwned,
 TotalChildren, Age, YearlyIncome,
 BikeBuyer
 FROM dbo.vTargetMail;'
 ,@input_data_1_name = N'TM'
 ,@params = N'@model VARBINARY(MAX) OUTPUT'
 ,@model = @model OUTPUT;
INSERT INTO dbo.dsModels (ModelName, Model)
VALUES('rxDT', @model);
GO
```

You can query the table to check whether the model was successfully stored:

```
SELECT *
FROM dbo.dsModels;
```

Now you can use the `PREDICT()` function to get the predictions:

```
DECLARE @model VARBINARY(MAX) =
(
 SELECT Model
 FROM dbo.dsModels
 WHERE ModelName = 'rxDT'
);
SELECT d.CustomerKey, d.Age, d.NumberCarsOwned,
 d.BikeBuyer, p.BikeBuyer_Pred
FROM PREDICT(MODEL = @model, DATA = dbo.vTargetMail AS d)
WITH(BikeBuyer_Pred FLOAT) AS p
ORDER BY d.CustomerKey;
```

Here are a few lines from the result. The predicted value above `0.50` means a predicted bike buyer. Note that there are some incorrect predictions already in these lines:

```
CustomerKey Age NumberCarsOwned BikeBuyer BikeBuyer_Pred
----------- --- --------------- --------- ----------------
11000       31  0               1         0.680851063829787
11001       27  1               1         0.424242424242424
11002       32  1               1         0.424242424242424
11003       29  1               1         0.636594663278272
11004       23  4               1         0.241935483870968
```

You can use the following code to clean up the `AdventureWorkDW2017` demo database:

```
DROP TABLE IF EXISTS dbo.TMTrain;
DROP TABLE IF EXISTS dbo.TMTest;
DROP TABLE IF EXISTS dbo.dsModels;
GO
```

Summary

In this chapter, you learned about predictive models. You learned about linear regression, Naive Bayes, logistic regression, decision trees, decision forests, and gradient-boosting trees. You learned how to evaluate the models. Finally, you learned how to store the models in SQL Server and use them for native predictions.

And here we are, at the end of the book. Thank you for reading it. I really hope this book will help you on your path toward becoming a better data scientist.

Other Books You May Enjoy

If you enjoyed this book, you may be interested in these other books by Packt:

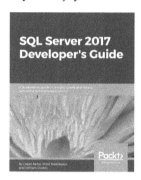

SQL Server 2017 Developer's Guide

Dejan Sarka, Miloš Radivojević, William Durkin

ISBN: 978-1-78847-619-5

- Explore the new development features introduced in SQL Server 2017
- Identify opportunities for In-Memory OLTP technology
- Use columnstore indexes to get storage and performance improvements
- Extend database design solutions using temporal tables
- Exchange JSON data between applications and SQL Server
- Use the new security features to encrypt or mask the data
- Control the access to the data on the row levels Discover the potential of R and Python integration
- Model complex relationships with the graph databases in SQL Server 2017

SQL Server 2017 Machine Learning Services with R
Tomaž Kaštrun, Julie Koesmarno

ISBN: 978-1-78728-357-2

- Get an overview of SQL Server 2017 Machine Learning Services with R
- Manage SQL Server Machine Learning Services from installation to configuration and maintenance
- Handle and operationalize R code
- Explore RevoScaleR R algorithms and create predictive models
- Deploy, manage, and monitor database solutions with R
- Extend R with SQL Server 2017 features
- Explore the power of R for database administrators

Leave a review - let other readers know what you think

Please share your thoughts on this book with others by leaving a review on the site that you bought it from. If you purchased the book from Amazon, please leave us an honest review on this book's Amazon page. This is vital so that other potential readers can see and use your unbiased opinion to make purchasing decisions, we can understand what our customers think about our products, and our authors can see your feedback on the title that they have worked with Packt to create. It will only take a few minutes of your time, but is valuable to other potential customers, our authors, and Packt. Thank you!

Index

URL 26
missing values
  about 91
  handling 91, 94, 95
ML services (In-Database) packages
  installing 146, 147, 148
mode 33
monotonic variable 66

N

Naive Bayes algorithm
  using 175, 177
native predictions 186
null hypothesis 119

O

object 33
object-oriented programming 45
oblique 165
observations 37
one-way ANOVA 135
ordinal variable 67
orthogonal 165

P

patterns 25
permissions 35
piecemeal linear regression 181
polynomial regression 141
predictions 25
predictive models
  evaluating 169, 174
  test set 169
  training set 169
principal component analysis (PCA)
  about 159, 163, 166
  factor analyses 162, 164
procedural programming 45
promax 165
python code
  writing 47, 49
Python environment
  selecting 46
Python
  Microsoft scalable libraries, leveraging 111

Q

quantiles 72
quartiles 72

R

R Tools for Visual Studio (RTVS) 26
R
  coding 28, 30
  data structures, using 37, 43
  dplyr package, using 112, 116
  learning 31, 35, 37
  obtaining 26
random forests algorithm 184
range 71
rank 67
real-time scoring 186
receiver operating characteristic (ROC) 174
recursive partitioning 181
regression trees 181
relative entropy 107
rotation 164
rules 25

S

scatterplot 87
sequences 31
sigmoid function 180
skewness 75, 76, 79
spread
  measuring 71
SQL Server Management Studio (SSMS)
  about 60
  URL 9
SQL Server Reporting Services (SSRS) reports 58
SQL Server
  installing 7
  integrating, with ML 58, 61
  setting up 8
standard deviation (σ) 73
standard normal distribution 75
subqueries 17
support 149

T

taildness 68
Transact-SQL (T-SQL)
  about 7
  predicting with 186, 188
true negatives 174
true positives 174

V

variables 32, 37
variables, types
  about 66
  continuous variables 66

discrete variables 67
variance 73
variance of a sample 73
variance of the population 73
varimax 165

W

weighted sum 180
window functions 18
workspace 30

Z

Z distribution 75

www.ingramcontent.com/pod-product-compliance
Lightning Source LLC
Chambersburg PA
CBHW080527060326
40690CB00022B/5053